Performing the *Gendered Self* in *Inter*cultural Communication

I0023496

Ozan Can Yılmaz

# Performing the *Gendered Self* in *Inter*cultural Communication

**PETER LANG**

**Bibliographic Information published by the
Deutsche Nationalbibliothek**
The Deutsche Nationalbibliothek lists this publication in the Deutsche
Nationalbibliografie; detailed bibliographic data is available online at
http://dnb.d-nb.de.

**Library of Congress Cataloging-in-Publication Data**
A CIP catalog record for this book has been applied for at the
Library of Congress.

ISBN 978-3-631-86076-2 (Print)
E-ISBN 978-3-631-86858-4 (E-PDF)
E-ISBN 978-3-631-86859-1 (EPUB)
10.3726/b19118

© Peter Lang GmbH
Internationaler Verlag der Wissenschaften
Berlin 2022
All rights reserved.

Peter Lang – Berlin · Bern · Bruxelles · Istanbul · New York · Oxford · Warszawa · Wien

This publication has been peer reviewed.

www.peterlang.com

# CONTENTS

# Preface

*"Every established order tends to produce the naturalization of its own arbitrariness" (Bourdieu 115)*

The intersectionality of culture, religion, and communication is integral to understanding the ways in which human subjects are socially constructed on the interplay of these three elements. It is through exploring the constitutive effects these three have on human subjectivities that we can more substantially comprehend how a subject is made into certain structures of being. While religious indoctrinations may have been seen as pivotal aspects of human culture, alternative approaches have emphasized on how religion suggests a culture in its own structuring. Moreover, the undeniable effect communication has on how individuals and communities conceptualize and transmit certain beliefs and practices is essential to understanding the interconnectedness of religion and culture. Thus, religious and cultural practices emerge from one another, which makes an intercultural dialogue a contested area over religious conceptualizations.

The consequential role of religious indoctrinations on gender is an incontrovertible phenomenon that is dogmatically constituting and perpetually reproducing the interactional patterns in which intercultural communication is substantiated. Similarly, the performances of social identities are not always contingent upon the relational dependency of the signifier to the signified social meaning, but there are multiplicities of interactional conflicts and symbolic interpretations that cause cross-cultural dialogues to continually merge and resolve in multiple decentered meanings. In this sense, intercultural communication in between distinct religious localities and dogmatic subjectivities is transpired within representational intricacies that arise from the dissimilar conceptualizations and marks of identity. In this regard, I seek to explore the essentialist role of the gendered hierarchies constituted through the rigorous enactment of institutionalized dogmatic power resulting in a religious scheme on gender. The gendered normativities fostered by religious indoctrinations on the feminine and masculine roles of men and women are can be explicitly seen in many aspects of intercultural communication. Thus, I am interested in the limits of religious observances in the acknowledgment and performance of restrictive, sexist, and phallo-centric norms of gender. For this purpose, I invite you to an exploration of the communicational complexities that stem from the dissimilarities of cultural conceptions on gender and distinctive marks of religious gender identity. In this book, I have sought to address the interactional roadblocks in the processes of social and cultural integration as well as to lay emphasis on the limits of confusion, anxiety, and uncertainty in cross-cultural contacts.

# CHAPTER ONE    Intersectional Definitions of Identity and Communication

> *Maybe the target nowadays is not to discover what we are, but to refuse what we are. We have to promote new forms of subjectivity through the refusal of this kind of individuality which has been imposed on us for several centuries (Foucault 216).*

There are several aspects that affect the nature of intercultural communication, and some of these aspects suggest a much broader area of influence than the others. Varying from ethnocentrism, stereotyping, and assumptions to racism, sexism, and education level, intercultural communication is challenged in various ways, and the study of communicational hindrances is crucial to overcoming these roadblocks for effective intercultural interactions. Considering how the clash of identities occurs across civilizations and societies influencing the global agenda of politics, economy, cultural growth, and globalization, similarly the religious dogmas on gender roles as a part of one's identity manifest its infallible and absolute nature through intercultural contact, which in many cases leads to anxiety, distress, confusion, and misconceptions. Traditional gender roles are enforced by the use of media, educational tools, social systems, and most dogmatically and powerfully religious indoctrinations. It can be seen in the dogmatic teachings of prominent religions that mothers are portrayed as the main caregivers to their children, women as submissive figures in many aspects of life, and men as leaders and clergies. Catholicism, for instance, only permits cisgender men to serve as priests and leaves no room for alternative gender identities (Johnson and Repta 17–39). More examples of authoritarian hegemony of religion over religious identity and gender roles can be seen in minority groups integrating into distinct societies as each member of the minority groups acts on predefined gender representations as expected by the normative indoctrination of the group they are affiliated with. Thus, it is not only the visible signs of communication that pose an obstacle in communication but also the performance of gendered beliefs that is a crucial aspect in intercultural dialogues.

One of the historical contributions of religion to the constitution of cultures has been through the social construction of gender roles. It is of significant importance to understand that there is a direct connection between the text and the current norm that the current norm could not have been born from any other phenomenon. Major religions like Christianity, Judaism, and Hinduism all separately propagate vastly different gender roles in their philosophical texts, and people of different societies have adopted and normalized those same gender roles in contemporary societies. It has been argued that when two parties have the same understanding of gender, communication flourishes, on the contrary, their different interpretations of gender prevent communication from flourishing. In this regard, the role of religious dogmatism in communicational processes can be seen through the interactional limitations and hindrances that occur when two people come in contact with one another while the normative and dogmatic expressions of verbal and nonverbal communication can prevent the interaction from flowing. Cultural differences are much more apparent in intercultural environments, and the diversified cultural representations trigger divergent communication manners. The dissimilarities of communicational behaviors and attributions can be enhanced through the involvement of the particularities of identity expressions, meaning that certain roles attributed to the identities of gender are manifested and performed in communication. Therefore, dogmatic genderization of interactional behaviors and their social performances in communication processes suggest substantially complex cross-cultural contacts.

The role of religion in the intersubjective construction of gender roles has been a notable phenomenon in analyzing the social construction of gendered attributions and behaviors. The historical dogmatic evolvement of gender roles has significantly evolved out of the biblical figures occurring throughout the scriptural narratives and the gendered deities fostering specific gender roles that eventually affect the conceptions of gender identities across cultures. Thus, I argue that an extensive analysis on the ancient sacred texts helps us understand the underlying reasons why some gendered conceptions, behaviors, and religious norms have been passed down the generations still being immensely impactful on intercultural integration. Because communication is an area for identity to be represented, the religious contribution to identity construction can be seen in the ways that the communicators choose certain interactional roles, behaviors, vocabulary, and nonverbal signs over others that represent their group belongings and religious collective identities.

We all tend to take on multiple social identities that define who we are through our interactions. It is for this reason that we almost innately manifest a natural and often inevitable tendency to identify ourselves with a multitude of social groups including those of gender and religion. Considering how institutionalized interpretations, beliefs, and conventional significations shape the ways in which an identity is formed, this book aims to address the interactional signs of gender within cross-cultural contacts. Because religious formations readily provide and impose its normative codes of interaction, I explore the normative conceptualizations made upon the performance of gender identities.

This book seeks to provide a comprehensive insight into the argument that dogmatic conceptualizations constitute gender roles and identities, and that intercultural communication is significantly shaped by religious gendered representations since each gendered subject in a given cultural locality is represented by those cultural aspects constituted by dogmatic indoctrinations. Throughout this book, elements of certain aspects of biblical indoctrinations are discussed for their role in the intercultural integration of religious gender identities. Besides, it is pivotal to empha-size on the argument that my attempt is to make a stronger emphasis on how dogmatic gendered conceptions encourage or hinder the processes of intercultural communication than the connection between gender roles, religion, and intercultural communication as distinct concepts. In my con-ceptualization of the subject, I problematize the intersectionality of gender, religion and communication by raising the following question: a) *"To what extent does the gendered dogma subjugate the subjective human agency over interactional marks of identity?"*

I would also like to refer to the academic objective and significance of the subject; to explore the socio-religious roadblocks for intercultural com-munication competency, to shed light on the underlying reasons for why certain cross-cultural interactions are immensely challenged while others remain effective. Considering the relational dependency between the social performance of gender and cross-cultural integration, the exploration of dogmatic aspects of gender could potentially suggest a cutting-edge understanding for communication studies.

It is of significant importance to provide some conceptualizations of the terms widely used throughout the book, and to lay out the conceptual basis for the primary research. Within the scope of this book, certain aspects of social identity are discussed based upon two major categories of identity; *the intersectionality of gender and religious identities.* Social identity can be defined as how a person would define himself depending on his group affiliations. Henri Tajfel's research on social identity suggests that the social groups we belong to create a sense of pride and confidence, which inevitably manifests itself in intercultural dialogues (Tajfel 33–47). Social identity can also be referred as the image we strive to enhance in order to consolidate our self-image. In this book, I discuss how a particular social belonging is performed in intercultural contact, and whether or not the performance of it hinders or encourages the communication processes (McLeod et al.).

Gender identity is referred as a socially constructed and non-essentialist concept. Gender, as conceptualized by West and Zimmerman, is a creative process whereby interactions with people and social groups help the formation of one's gender. Because verbal and nonverbal signs are the means to perform gender, communication can be approached as a complex process rather than being bidirectional and consistent (West et al. 127). Within the social constructionist aspects of gender, the normative roles of gender are unremittingly constituted and reproduced within cultural boundaries. The naturalization of gendered roles assigned to the sex binary also takes place within socio-cultural localities. As well as gender is constructed on a social and cultural scale, subgroups within broader cultural settings can also formulate their normative gendered ideals, which forms the main interest of this book.

Historical events such as reformation and enlightenment ramified the idea that religion had long remained as one's cultural ascription by birth rather than being a personally made decision (Grant 1–20). Shifting from perceiving religion as *a mere coincidence* a person happens to be born into towards *a matter of choice,* separating religion from its profound connections to the traditions and privatizing it to a more pluralistic worldview may affect the prevalence of dogmatic religious identities (Horsley et al. 1–48) However, this book seeks to make an emphasis on individuals and members whose religious affiliations are still inseparable from their identity performances despite all the attempts to personalize and privatize the religious identity.

Besides, it is pivotal to understand the concept of tolerance as the lack of it within certain religious occurrences may entangle and thwart the intercultural communication competency (Williams 430). The lack of communication competency stemming from the intolerant indoctrinations eventually creates dogmatic religious groups that have their own cosmology of being. Though this largely may concern the study of religious cults where closed groups encircled with certain doctrinal fences are discussed, there is still a considerable correlation between threatening cults and mainstream religious groups in their impenetrable and unquestionable indoctrinations made towards the identity formations of the member individuals (Saleem).

The distrust towards *the other* that can be said to begin from the early phases of religious involvement may also cause an obstacle in the subsequent interactions with the world outside and the cultural others in it (Arweck et al. 67–88). Because there is a distinguishable difference between religiosity and religious identity, it is necessary to state the argument that one's religious identity may arise from the particularities of his or her upbringing, and that it may not necessarily show the person's religiosity. However, contrary to such nominal religious identities, I am more interested in with those dogmatic subjectivities that willingly practice a belief, and that their whole structuring of inter-subjective interactions is almost always shaped in alignment with their faith (King et al. 431–456). Considering how there has been made a remarkable emphasis on the contribution of nationality and ethnicity on the formation of social identities, similarly the religious identity along with the particularities of the sectarian gendered conceptions play a tremendous role in how individual identities are enacted, socialized, and manifested within the practices of the every-day.

Studies that eventually involve the religious aspects in the social construction of identity have now been more visible in academia, still mainly exploring the differences arising from the sex binary of male and female performance of religiousness (King et al. 2–6). On the other hand, a more attentive academic intention is much needed to the hegemonic domains of the male-centric ideologies of men who enjoy the 'sacred' patriarchies through androcentric religious indoctrinations (Lee 369–384). In this sense,

I would like to refer to the concept of religion as a fundamental dogmatic aspect of human life, which can be defined as *"A set of beliefs concerning the cause, nature, and purpose of the universe, especially when considered as the creation of a superhuman agency or agencies, usually involving devotional and ritual observances, and often containing a moral code governing the conduct of human affairs"* (Robinson) while a similar conceptualization suggests that *"It is apparent that religion can be seen as a theological, philosophical, anthropological, sociological, and psychological phenomenon of human kind. To limit religion to only one of these categories is to miss its multifaceted nature and lose out on the complete definition"* (Robinson).

# CHAPTER TWO   Theories of Communication, Culture and Identity

## A. Re-Reading of Communication Theories

It is essential to understand that the study of human interactions is directly connected to the study of culture. Academic research conducted in relation to intercultural communication may consist of study areas such as *"attitudes, beliefs, cognition, language and linguistics, nonverbal cues, perceptions, stereotypes, thought-patterning and values"* as suggested in the Encyclopedia of Communication (Littlejohn, 248–250). In His book *The Cultural Dialogue (*Prosser 10–344), Michael E. Prosser explored the role of conflict and conflict resolution in a way that communication is an interactional means to control making use of power. Therefore, intercultural communication is vastly influenced by the power mechanisms of social control, and the development of cross-cultural interactions is highly impacted by the hegemonic power use and normative control mechanisms that may significantly emerge out of the religious implementations (Raven, 161–186).

*Communication Accommodation Theory* developed by Howard Giles has an important significance in analyzing how intercultural interactions are structured around the manner of speech, vocal patterns, and gestures relevant to the identity performance (Turner and West 492). The theory provides an in-depth insight into the different reasons why individuals tend to highlight or reduce the social differences between themselves through verbal and nonverbal communication. In this sense, the theory suggests a significant insight into why certain cross-cultural interaction patterns are used, and why the differences and similarities are pushed forward in intercultural communication (Xu 884–87). The theory is concerned with the intergroup and interpersonal factors that cause a modification in interaction manner proposing the idea that macro/micro-context social and cultural concerns influence communicational behaviors (Giles and Ogay 293).

The theory argues for two accommodation processes. One of them is *"Convergence"* that refers to individuals choosing to adapt to each other's communicative behaviors to minimize the social differences (Giles and Ogay 293). Convergence can take place through the use of verbal language and nonverbal marks, and *"when communicators are attracted to others, they will converge in their conversations,"* as argued by Turner and West (Turner and West 492). The reason that lies behind one's intention to converge can be given as the person's desire for social approval, and the more the desire for social approval is, the higher the levels of convergence are (Giles and Smith 45–65). In the context of intercultural communication, convergence means more effective communication that lifts off the barriers of uncertainty and interpersonal anxiety (Giles and Coupland 1–68). Communication accommodation theory has been widely applied to intercultural communication for its connection to interpersonal, inter-group, and inter-ethnic communication (Anderson and Ross 20–50). As further laid out in the chapter four, there may be a certain level of inclination toward convergence and to the behavioral norms of the new habitat, which may be the result of an awareness for the norms of living of a new cultural locality that enables an effective socio-behavioral convergence and integration process (Gallois and Callan 245–269). On the other hand, the theory suggests another form of accommodation that was referred as *over-accommodation*. Sensory over-accommodation, dependency over-accommodation, and intergroup over-accommodation are the three different forms over-accommodation can take place in. I am more concerned with intergroup over-accommodation that argues for the idea that people are manipulated based on a general stereotype. Intergroup over-accommodation is when speakers tend to situate listeners within certain cultural groups without acknowledging individual uniqueness. Here we see socially categorized stereotypes that individuals or groups have for others, and definitions by which people define their environment creating a socio-cognitive form of detraction for the communication process. On a larger scale, this form of over-accommodation can be applied to how belief systems can potentially formulate certain definitions and stereotypes that may cause a cognitive process of divergence or damage for the effectiveness of the intercultural communication. Socially constructed and categorized gender representations may stem from dogmatic ideologies, and thus these gendered dogmas foster certain normative roles of gender, which ultimately cause a certain form of over-accommodation and defamation to an interaction process (Turner and West 492). Another form crucial to explore is *divergence* that makes an emphasis on linguistic differences whereby a sense of distinctiveness from the other is created. This aspect causes individuals to maintain their in-group language sustaining the affiliated social identity (Giles and Coupland 1–68). It can be applied into areas where one's religious identity dictates certain discursive power hierarchy demanding another one less powerful, which eventually causes divergence in the process of one's cultural integration (Giles and Ogay 293).

A Schematic Representation of AUM Theory from Gudykunst, *"An Anxiety/Uncertainty Management (AUM) Theory of Effective Communication: Making the Mesh of the Net Finer"* proposes categories such as *'Social Categorization of Strangers'* with positive expectations, perceived personal similarities, and understanding group differences. It further suggests *'Ethical Interactions'* with maintaining dignity, moral inclusiveness, and respect for strangers. It also suggests *'Reactions to Strangers'* with empathy, tolerance for ambiguity, and rigid intergroup attitudes, and *'Self-Concept'* with social identities, personal identities, and collective self-esteem (Griffin 426–38). Out of these categories, certain ones such as maintaining dignity, moral inclusiveness, and tolerance for ambiguity are crucial as these elements form a significant part of the integration process of those challenged through the social collision of identities. In this sense, I argue that an interactional effort to maintain dignity could either be a stumbling block or a way to gain respect for the processes of communication (Cragan and Shields 274–276). Similarly, the level of tolerance toward ambiguous lifestyles of strangers could also suggest a sound level of *mindfulness* (Gudykunst 282). Thus, preventing possible misconceptions and misunderstandings during an interaction is a hard thing to achieve especially when there is a clash of cultural conceptions. It is for this reason that the theory suggests anxiety and uncertainty to be the underlying reasons for intercultural misconceptions, arguing for the necessity of a balance of anxiety and uncertainty in social situations (Griffin 426–38).

Considering how individual beliefs may hinder or encourage an effective intercultural communication depending on the cultural context, the interactional norms of culture people use to communicate can also be considered as fostered by religious affiliations (Gudykunst 3–25). In this regard, it is worth mentioning the name Georg Simmel who suggested *"The concept of social type as being cast by the specifiable reactions and expectations of others"* (Simmel 1950). This concept proposes the presence of certain behavioral dissimilarities toward certain groups and individuals of distinct backgrounds. The concept suggests *the idea of a stranger* who never belongs to the group from the very beginning until the end of the interaction process. (Wolff 402–408). Thus, the concept of a social type perceived as a stranger brings up certain issues in the process of cross-cultural integration. Moreover, individual stance on morality and faith may reinforce personal conceptions on social type as a stranger, and a stranger whose cultural and religious background vary from the local group norms could have difficulty performing certain identity marks. Based on the axioms proposed by Gudykunst, to reduce the level of anxiety, there is a need for increasing *"the degree to which our social identities guide our interactions if our social identities are secure"* (Gudykunst 302–303), suggesting that higher levels of self-esteem eventually decrease our anxiety (Gudykunst 1–28). In this sense, the social identity theory developed by Henri Tajfel argues that *"formal participation within a given social group would enhance individuals' social identities regarding that group"* (Greenfield and Marks 245–259), while the term social identity is defined as *"the knowledge that (one) belongs to certain social groups together with some emotional and value significance of the group membership"* (Tajfel 272–302).

Considering the argument also proposed by Emile Durkheim that is religious beliefs and practices can be seen both as an individual and group level phenomenon, all social categories shaped by individual religious practices could help to construct a self-concept which eventually could guide our social interactions in our integration processes (Greenfield 245–259). Hence, our secured social identities and level of self-esteem constructed within collective religious formations may suggest certain rigidity and determinism for intercultural communication. Considering how social interactions can be significantly affected by individual concepts of social identity as formed by religious indoctrinations, such condition of social interactions may trigger certain gender performance that could result either in an effective communication or in the hindrance for cross-cultural integration (Berger and Calabrese 99–112).

The research in *Global Missiology* conducted by George Yip explores the areas whereby cross-cultural missionaries are hindered or encouraged in their interactions with locals. In the research, it is argued that individuals or groups with certain religious identities moving to mission fields where intercultural communication competencies are needed can be challenged in their integration processes (Spitzberg 7–24). Similarly, the concept of *collective self-esteem* through a sense of confidence in group affiliations may turn into lower levels of self-esteem, one that socially isolates the person by restraining within the religious boundaries. As such may hinder the person from performing contextual and culturally appropriate marks of interaction, and may cause communicational misconceptions (Yip 2010). The reactions to strangers has a significant importance in one's ability *"to process complex information about strangers, flexibility of attitude, tolerance of ambiguity, and empathy"* (Gudykunst 255–256), which enables us not to perceive strangers merely as cognitive beings, and to get rid of fixed attitudes that cause *"ethnocentrism, stereotyping, and prejudice"* (Gudykunst 298, 1–28). Likewise, it is relevant to mention the effort of in-groups to categorize the out-groups into definitions that make sense to them, and it is in this sense that the concept of stereotyping comes into the scene. In Simmel's concept of social type, it is seen that both negative and positive behavioral expectations on strangers may cause anxiety and may lead one to avoidance in interaction (Simmel 8–34). On the other hand, solutions for coping up with high levels of uncertainty and anxiety in intercultural communication are crucial (Yip 2010). Thus, the term *mindfulness* proposes a new category through which strangers are perceived much more openly, and their culturally distinct signs of interaction are more appreciated (Langer 62).

Steve J. Kulich proposes *"a nine multi-level analysis of culture model for future cross-cultural research"* portraying culture *"as propagated mythic ideals,"* *"as expected behavior mechanics,"* *"as mediated metaphors,"* and *"as personalized meaning"* (Littlejohn and Karen 248–50). His arguments on cross-cultural communication leads us to our main area of inquiry that cross-cultural research on an inter-group and thus intercultural scale is significantly correlated with the propagated myths that form the limits and definitions of gender identity and roles. Individual performances of certain communicational codes of interaction formed by religious belongings and *inherited metaphors* and symbolic constructions of gendered ideals that reinforce religious identities are two crucial aspects to consider with regard to the flow of intercultural contacts.

Gudykunst and Lee suggest a five-approach understanding to *"incorporate culture into communication theories,"* and one of these approaches is the function of communication theories *"as creating culture"* (Xu 884–887). This particular approach argues that communicational manners fostered in certain in-group activities and in the particularities of language could eventually create its interactional subculture (Lee et al. 373–387). Communication theories function *"to generate explanation for communication between people from different cultures or to explain how communication varies across cultures"*, and it is also suggested that cross-cultural studies *"in addition to standard social science methods such as logical consistency, explanatory power, and parsimony"* should also include *"more than one dimension of cultural variability, linking dimensions of cultural variability directly with the cultural norms and rules that influence the communication behavior being explained"* (Xu 884–887). This suggestion provides us a research insight to avoid the oversimplification of group behaviors also enabling us to see the intercultural and inter-group signs of interactions within their cultural context. Thus, communication in its function *to create the culture itself* and the complexities in communicational definitions that are contingent on dogmatic ideologies demand a more complex and multi-faceted approach to the research of cross-cultural integration.

Concerning the idiosyncrasies constructed by one's acknowledgement of certain norms of identity, a communication process in-between human subjects of distinct normative conceptualizations may cause violations of social and cultural norms. Approaching to intercultural communication as an exchange of behaviors and clash of dissimilar code of conducts, the *Expectancy Violations Theory* by Judee Burgoon offers a wider perspective to why and how one's behavior can violate another person's expectations in an interaction process (Burgoon et al. 58–79). Considering that expectancies are majorly and commonly built upon socially constructed norms and the characteristics of an affiliated social identity, our expectancies may be constituted by pre-existing concepts of thought consisting of the normative schemes (58–79). Thus, communicational expectancies can be argued to be socially constructed within certain dogmatic normativities.

The discrepant and divergent cultures converging on a common interactional ground may conduce to undesired and violated communicational expectancies, which causes a communicative predicament (Griffin 84–92). In other words, *a receiver perceives or expects of the sender's behavior not as an arbitrary choice but rather as noticeably deliberate.* The theory proposes two major expectancies; *prescriptive* and *predictive* (Houser 217–218). Religious formations within their own cultural distinctiveness can be said to set up norms and rules of behavior considered the most typical of that particular group, which is referred as the predictive expectations. On the other hand, the beliefs upon which set of behaviors ought to be performed and what's intended by the communicator form the prescriptive behaviors (217–218). These beliefs on the limits of human behavior, when considering in the context of social identity, arise from the idea that there are certain behavioral allowances and prohibitions made upon the human subject.

Intercultural communication strongly depends on the level of each communicator's condition of integration toward social and cultural localities. Thus, every interactional process is scaled on the individual ability to handle communicational anxiety and uncertainties. This has been the primary focus of Young Yun Kim in her *Cross-Cultural Adaptation Theory* that explores the processes of stress adaptation and growth (Kim 3–10). Her research points out to the argument that confronting new patterns of interaction increases the level of anxiety, and gives the person a sense of confusion generating from his or her habitual beliefs and conceptions on appropriate interactional behaviors in communication. Defense mechanisms can be utilized to reduce negative stress while self-defense may result in person's resistant behaviors to maintain the communicational habits, which ultimately affect the growth in cross-cultural integrations (3–10). Although there may be an observable shift in the individual's willingness to integrate into the new cultural settlement, this is, however, significantly challenged through habitual insistence on the performance of certain social identity markers because the otherwise is acknowledged and perceived as a threat to identity. The theory deals also with the idea that cross-cultural integration processes may change from one individual to another depending on their willingness to negotiate in-between dissimilar cultural practices (Kim 283–300). Similarly, it suggests that the polycultural cognitive structures in the conceptual mind of the human subject may result in the formation an intercultural identity, which replaces the conventional conceptions of the self and the otherness with a more universalized form of understanding (283–300). Conversely, we could consider why some may prefer to remain in their culturally constructed comfort-zones resisting the change that intercultural interactions may entail.

I argue that religious institutionalism suggests a) *certain constitutive mechanisms that formulate subtle ways of dogmatically guiding the behavioral patterns of the member individuals,* b) *a meta-communication defining the limits of interactional encoding and decoding* c) *indoctrinations of delimitative ideologies that encircle the members within a closed system blocking out alternative aspects of social and cultural being.* Considering how such devotional levels of surrender to an ideology encapsulates the believer in the hope of collective belongingness, it causes counterfeit complacency and a sense of contentment as long as the believer remains inside the dogmatic realm. Thus, it becomes pertinent to link this argument to what the theory explores; *the velocity of a successfully achieved adaptation process* (Kim 15–40). Though the theory further discusses the possibilities around an identity transformation for enabling pluralistic interactions, I am much more concerned with the resistance shown against plurality in communication due to stringent identity performances (Kim 3–10).

The U-Curve model, developed by Kalvero Oberg, focuses on the emotional upheavals caused by intercultural communication. It suggests that one's integrational journey in a host culture begins with high motivations but drops down after the 'honeymoon' process is over. It makes the person compromise many things, familiarizes the person to new codes of conduct, and makes some adjustments for an effective cultural settlement (Kalvero).

An adaptation process is rather a psychological condition possibly causing the person to face communicational discomfort and anxiety. Similarly, sociocultural adaptation refers to the period in which the person learns how to interact with the members of the hosting society including the acquisition of culture-specific communication skills. According to the salient models of cultural adaptation, acquiring a wider understanding of the values, beliefs, and norms practiced and exalted in the hosting culture is also a part of the sociocultural adaptation. A similar model, *the transition model,* developed by William Bridges, proposes three phases, one of which concerns the possibility of anxiety and skepticism that may take place in one's cultural adjustment process (Bridges 1–8). All these models above-mentioned are highly connected to the idea that *communication is a ramified multi-dimensional process that comprises of sociocultural and psychological adaptation roadblocks demanding a proper management of anxiety, confusion, and integrative skills.* The acculturative stress theory (Ausubel 617–631) has been developed to provide reasons for stress reactions stemming from the person's experiences with cultural assimilation. The theory suggests that such stress often consists of having to balance between the individual values and the values of the new cultural locality (Lueck 186–195).

In this regard, it is absolutely worth mentioning the term *acculturation* as it refers to social and cultural blending, and that acculturation process often demands a relatively drastic change in the individual's conception of socio-cultural aspects (Sam et al. 472). The process of acculturation primarily entails immigrants, and concerns issues around cultural pluralism, while certain religious groups is more concerned about socio-cultural detachment or separatism than integration (Zhou 975–1008).

Integrative communication theory (Kim 15–40) was developed by Young Yun as a theory of cross-cultural adaptation, and it argues for the idea that the solution to a more integrative intercultural communication would be through one's willingness to let go of the characteristics of his or her culture of origin. The theory exploring the processes deculturation and acculturation (Kim 435–453) stands out as an alternative model that explores the connections between individual beliefs and values and the communication processes affected by them. The model suggests that the more time spent in the host culture, the more likely one's incorporation with the local environment becomes stronger. In the end, *the re-structuring of the cognitive schemes begins,* and the person's perceptions and views become adjusted to the new culture (Kim 66–77). This process argued by the model, however, is fundamentally challenged by the norms imposed by the certain in-group formations, which leaves out the settlement in an out-group environment.

The mentally conditioned individual is encouraged to remain intact and celibate in his or her behavioral condition, and thus appears to be unwilling to accept mental transition into new cultural conceptions. Kim also deals with the term *intercultural identity* (Kim 1992), which means to go beyond the culture of origin by being receptive to new cultural aspects. The theorist asserts the idea that *"Communication is crucial to acculturation. It*

*provides the fundamental means by which individuals develop insights into
their new environment"* (Kim 66–77). For this reason, reducing uncertainty
and anxiety would be crucial in acquiring acculturation: *"In uncertainty/
anxiety reduction theory, anxiety and attributional confidence are said to
be the basic causes of intercultural adaptation"* (Gudykunst 106–139).
Likewise, *the developmental model of intercultural sensitivity* by Milton
Bennett comes up with concrete steps of an acculturation process. The
model suggests that one's initial contact with a new cultural environment
often manifests itself as denial, which is followed by interactional defense
mechanisms. Following denial, the processes of minimization, acceptance,
adaptation, and eventually integration take place in intercultural communication. In chapter four, relevant primary research is shown for the areas
where these steps are left out, challenged or strictly followed.

Besides the sociological and psychological components discussed above,
there is also the processes of individual cognitive acquisition. Social identification functions collaboratively with the cognitive processes and
perceptions such as *"how individuals or groups view themselves and the
effects of stereotypes and discrimination on their identity"* (Adler 13–23).
Cognitive framework mainly refers to the transitioning and shifting processes of social and cultural identities, which can either be avoided or inevitably manifested. Concerning the idea that one's social identification can
be subject to constant change, *the transitional experience model* developed
by Peter S. Adler lays an emphasis on the changes that arise in one's identity marks during cultural shift and adaptation. The model proposes the
idea that following the initial contact with the new culture, confusion,
disorientation, and disintegration come. Through these chaotic feelings,
one becomes aware of the differences in beliefs, norms, and values in
the host culture. This condition either results in the individual's refusal
of cultural integration or in the acknowledgement of alternative cultural
representations (Adler 13–23).

Shalom Schwartz made his studies around the significance in exploring
the value systems that help us to understand the culture itself. Exalted
values affect and shape the communicational behaviors, resulting in the
emergence of a desired interactional code of conduct. The idea that a communicator may conceive the behaviors of the communicatee based on his or
her cultural values makes it more necessary to study the value dynamics in

a communication process. It is also worth referring to the idea that *"some of the most recent international and intercultural conflicts have been motivated by value differences"* (Schwartz 43–73). Analyzing cultures the way Schwartz verbalized it as *"rich complex of meanings, beliefs, practices, symbols, norms, and values prevalent among people in society,"* brings up three cultural dimensions as explained in his theory of value orientations (43–73). Out of these three dimensions, the notions of *autonomy vs. embeddedness* and *hierarchy vs. egalitarianism* are crucial to explore. The relation between the person and the group and the extent people are autonomous or embedded in their groups construct the first dimension. The embeddedness into a particular collectivity constitutes the very nature of religious formations, and the shared values, lifestyles, social relationships within dogmatic constitutions form ideal identity performances for the affiliated individuals (43–73). Significations over interactional situations and the processes of the formation of *meaning* are made through collectivist and communal embeddedness into a larger group. Thus, it can be said that the embedded cultures preserve the status quo by not making it subject to alteration, and therefore abstain from activities including communication processes that threaten the in-group fidelity and traditional order of things. The commitment to a rigid structuring of communicational significations as well as obedience to group normativities are two crucial aspects that maintain and reproduce the masculinist gendered roles and dogmatized social identities. In this sense, the concept of embeddedness fosters hegemonic significations on gender. Another aspect is the concept of hierarchy within a cultural construct. Hierarchical order that divinely operates within religious formations seeks to ensure the individual's dispossession on gender roles by expropriating identity so that the order may not be disrupted. Despite the unequal dispensation of identity roles within such hierarchically operating order, unquestionable compliance with non-agentive impositions of the roles of gender identity remain problematic (43–73).

## B. Gender and Identity: Bourdieusian Gender

Bourdieu's conceptualization of *habitus* refers to structured dispositions and propensities, which is said to be instilled in individuals through a *cultural programming*. Similarly, I am interested in the unremitting diffusion ideologies and constant socialization of identities in a way that it is not only the social but also the bodily identities are formed within the concept of habitus. Thus, the merging of the social and the physical constitute the subject through the concretization of gender ideals and the naturalization of the normative conceptions on femininity and masculinity (Kelly 3).

It is argued that "it is not just that the spatial is socially constructed; the social is spatially constructed too" (Massey, 1994). Thus, space and culture can be argued to have infused in one another. Considering space also as a cultural locality, the social reflections of gender can be immensely seen in the construction of spatial localities, and these localized gendered configurations tend to present us a certain set of *gendered dispositions* on human interactions. Social interactions within socialization processes are profoundly rooted in the *gendered habitus* through which the socially acceptable normative forms of gendered acting are implemented. It is to say that *"society becomes deposited in persons in the form of lasting dispositions, or trained capacities and structured propensities to think, feel and act in determinant ways, which then guide them"* (Wacquant, 2005). A sense of habitus emerges and subtly dictates what is socially implemented, which Bourdieu describes as *"in this sense, habitus is created and reproduced unconsciously, without any deliberate pursuit of coherence, without any conscious concentration"* (Bourdieu, 1984). It is then relevant to argue that a prevailing religious ideology that has dogmatic implications on gender comes along with the social and cultural manifestation of hegemonic masculinities as well as the social seclusion and dogmatic subjugation of women to the predominant androcentric normativities. It is within such habitus of the gendered performances of the body that human interactions are substantiated on reproduced normativities and structured propensities.

In this regard, I argue that inter-subjective interactions consisting of distinct cultural localities can be formed by the dogmatic infusion of the structured signs of verbal and nonverbal marks of identity. However, human agency cannot be thrown out; in spite of the rigidity and essentialism of religious constructions of identity, *gender has a remarkably distinct function to diminish its own dogmas to re-establish itself in a new form of expression.* Thus, gender perpetually emerges despite the stringent constraints any ideology may force, which is contingent on the deconstructive will of the subject and the limits of the subversion of identity.

## 1. Performative Subjectivation of Gender

In exploring the dynamics of gender, I would also like to include some of the crucial aspects formulated by the Butlerian conceptualization of gender. Dogmatic significations of gender suggest a binary conception in the construction of gender, which is either by nature or birth; it argues for *a passive code* on one's body excluding the subjective agency and the sociocultural evolvement of gender. Her approach vis-à-vis the normative systemization of gender lays an emphasis of the socio-cultural process in which gender emerges. Interested in the concept of gender as a performative act, I argue it is also the presence of the social taboo and prohibitions that forcefully construct a performative gender act (Butler 519–531). Butler argues that *"gender is not a radical choice... [nor is it] imposed or inscribed upon the individual"* (519–531). The essentialist basis for gender dogmatism argues that it is the normative acting of gender through human interactions that has served the emergence of androcentric social orders, which legitimized the sex binary (519– 531).

The sex binary imposed by the interests of the religious hegemony demands distinctive and exclusionary separations between the categories of gender identity, eliminating the alternative ways of gendering being. Considering that there is no *'original identity prior to repetition,'* (519– 531), imitational and repetitive aspect of gender performance help sustain the absolute institutional hegemony over the identities of gender. The regulative dogmatic discourse on gender identity suggests a *socially manifest ritualization* of the gendered ideals through human interactions, which fosters dogmatically structured conventionalities of gender. These idealized rituals substantiated on human identity explicitly intrusively re-structures the social construction of the gendered roles (Butler 95). As a consequence of such gender roles vis-à-vis dissimilar performances of gender, communication faces socio-cultural obstructions that may conduce to intercultural shame, religious violence, ostracism, and social exclusion.

# CHAPTER THREE    Sacred Impositions on Gender

*"So God created man in his own image, in the image of God he created him; male and female he created them." (Genesis 1:27)*

## A. Identities in Collision

Identity has an undeniably significant role in our intercultural dialogues as it operates as a bridge between communication and culture. Communication is a dynamic medium through which we come to a broader understanding of our identities. It functions both as a verbal and nonverbal means of expression in which social identities are represented. External perceptions of our identity performances and our actual intentions in the expressions of who we think we are may collide with one another, and it is in such collision that a communication process inevitably becomes a battle ground for the clashing of identities. It is through the expressive emergence of identities in communication that the desired impression is carried forward, expressed, co-created, and challenged (Hecht et al. 199–235). Thus, *the distinctive expressions of identities become more evident within the dissimilarities of a contextually remote setting of communication as well as through the divergent signs of interaction of disparate identities.*

On the other hand, the communicational similarities in the performances of identities may eliminate the sense of insecurity. For instance, in case of a physical or emotional attraction between communicators, it can be argued that the sexual orientation and the gender identity have more cruciality than the national or ethnical identities. The idea that we all are innately subject to multiplicities of identities and that we continue to assume different marks of identity manifest through our interactional processes, perceptual significations as well as conceptual categorizations on identity are vital to the functionality of intercultural communication.

Considering how the term *heterosexual* has had multiple allocated significations over time, the conceptual shift in the definition of the term shows us how it no longer connotes a person who has sexual intercourse

with both sexes. The term evolved around various social meanings beginning from the earlier times when it meant an emphasis on procreation and
female submissiveness (Katz 33–83). It is in this sense that we can approach
the possible implications of a gender identity as a concept of *perpetual
becoming* and *a concept that reproduces its own undoing*. Such doing of
gender vis-à-vis its unremitting evolvement emerges from within the social
interactionalism through communicative marks of identity.

While the misuse or insufficient expression of identity marks may conduce to in-group conflict, which later may result in social exclusion and
dysphoria (Shaffer), the same interactional marks of identity, both verbal
and nonverbal, operates as a means to manifest where we collectively
belong. The identity marks we carry in our speech and nonverbal expression
convey a message, and we know whom we are interacting with based on
the assumptions we have about these codes of identity the person performs.
Gender and religious identities, in particular, carry a more symbolic and
symbiotic coding; it is full of identity specific expressions and consists of
unique verbal and nonverbal signs. Nakayama expressed a similar point
of view *"Who am I perceived to be when I communicate with others? My
identity is very much tied to the ways in which others speak to me and the
ways in which society represents my interests"* (Nakayama 14).

## 1. At the Intersection of Power and Knowledge

> *"The world is covered with signs that must be deciphered, and those signs, which
> reveal resemblances and affinities, are themselves no more than forms of simili-
> tude. To know must therefore be to interpret: to find a way from the visible mark
> to that which is being said by it and which, without that mark, would lie like
> unspoken speech, dormant within things"* (Foucault 375–380).

I consider it necessary to include some crucial aspects of the intersectionality
of power and knowledge mainly referring the concepts developed by the
Foucauldian discourse. His conceptual analysis emphasizes the power
relationships in a society, and his conceptualizations are essentially pertinent to the idea that how ecclesiastical or confessional language functions
to display power mechanisms infused in the everyday interactions of the
members of a society. The institutional power enforced by the possessors of
a subjugating autonomy fosters *a systematically structured language within*

*the spheres of dogmatic encoding and decoding displaying the hegemonic power.* Such hegemonic display of power becomes evident in our every-day practices of human interactions as well as through the structures of communicative language. Thus, a *communicative cosmos of being* is dictated for the interactional performances of preliminary composed marks of identity.

Considering power as the manifestation and disclosure of knowledge, *the evolvement of power within a given religious structure of knowledge seeks to subdue the episteme in which the human existence is structured.* It further begets to *an absolutist ontology encircling the human subject within the existential particularities of its own spiritual cosmos.* The Christian Church, as an institutionalized power, has held *a long-standing culturally consecrated hegemony as well as subtle means of social domination* over the believing communities. Foucault's conceptualization of '*the exercise of confession*' is relevant to see how an ecclesiastical practice operates as a means to claim ownership of knowledge, and more significantly gives birth to new forms of knowledge. Because the truth-telling through confessions creates *truthful knowledge* and the knowledge is gained through the practice of power that the exercise of confession possesses, it can then be assumed that dogmatic power enforces a kind of knowledge that is both emergent and sustained through the spiritual devotion and surrender in our everyday practices. In other words, *a reckless surrender to the will of the divine and its represented presence here on earth; or a gentle sacred mechanism to subjugate the meek.*

In his discourse, gender identity remains inseparable from the forms of power: "*Through the confession of inner secrets truth becomes the means by which sex is manifested*" (Foucault 1–133). It is thus that *sex as a biological category is formed as a means of hegemonic power, rather than it being an essentialist part of human biology.* As Foucault saw the connection between power and knowledge not only as a constraint but also a medium through which new ways of thinking and acting unfold, I argue that the dogmatic hegemony over individual identities may result in the emergence of new marks of identity and unprecedented behaviors in communication. (1–133).

## 2. Judeo-Christian Influences on Gender

*"Christianity taught us to see the eye of the lord looking down upon us. Such forms of knowledge project an image of reality, at the expense of reality itself. They talk figures and icons and signs, but fail to perceive forces and flows. They bind us to other realities, and especially the reality of power as it subjugates us. Their function is to tame, and the result is the fabrication of docile and obedient subjects."* — Gilles Deleuze, Anti-Oedipus: Capitalism and Schizophrenia

Although I distinctively explore the Judeo-Christian aspects in this book, I would also like to include several contrastive aspects from outside the Judeo-Christianity. These contrastive examples are included so that we may see the similarity in the construction of gender roles even when they are formed in entirely different cultural localities. Ancient religious goddesses have been constructive figures in the creation of gender roles, meaning that the divine attributes of certain female deities have influenced the gender roles imposed on the non-divine. Different societies re-interpreted these deities to formulate an overall gender representation. The Nordic goddess *Freya,* for instance, used to represent love and war till her representation was changed to love and sexual behavior after centuries. The Hindu goddess *Kali* stands out as opposing the typical gendered role of women suggesting subversive roles for women. The conventional conceptions on what women should represent is significantly challenged as the stereotypical gender roles of women such as love, beauty, and fertility are exchanged with *Kali* representing the goddess of destructive war. On the other hand, there are examples of female deities representing the traditional female roles as in the case of the Greek goddess *Aphrodite* that represents vanity and beauty (Davidson).

The normative dogmatism on gender imposes a two-edged conception on sexual identity enforcing a binary structuring on gender performance. Such binarism is both formulated and sustained based on long-existing religious texts and figures in them. Admiration toward gendered deities and religious figures causes the formation of such marks of communicative behaviors that individuals who adopt them become symbolically re-constructed by religious antiquities. Thus, I argue for the presence of *a sense of interconnectedness between the ambiguous ancient past and the actual modern-day.*

In Abrahamic religions, the prophets whose life-time stories recorded in the scriptures are predominantly male with certain masculine aspects in common. There are plenty of recorded influential biblical figures, among these figures are Abraham, Moses, David, and Elijah, etc. These scriptural gendered figures reinforce the long-prevailing conventional conceptions of masculinity as well as the gender roles of an ideal male representation. These highly revered and consecrated biblical men also constitute certain communicational marks for those who look up to them, by serving the purpose of maintaining 'the manliness' of men as created by God. Abraham, for instance, represents obedience, faithfulness, and courage for the believing men while David, Elijah, and Moses are seen as role models for bravery and battle. In this regard, the complementarianism is a key term that suggests the idea that the headship roles belong to men whereas the support roles are linked to women (Wright 2004). Hence, it can be argued that the creation of men resulted in a set of masculine or manly behavioral attributes that have been passed down the generations through the oral traditions and sacred writings, which are still encouraged to be practiced among the modern-day believers.

It should be noted that the biblical interpretations of what is considered to be a godly man and woman form today's hierarchical structuring of church. Similarly, the apostles, who were all men of diverse backgrounds, have contributed to the overwhelmingly patriarchal and male-dominated hegemony of church resulting in the unequal positioning of women being placed mostly into the supporting positions. While catholicism takes pride in the influence the church fathers have had on both the formation of its doctrinal theology and church traditions, the crucial reality of the concept of church fathers along with the fact that the twelve disciples, apostles and all the popes have all been men cannot be underestimated in exploring the masculinist presence and male dominance in the governing of the Catholic church. *In this story told by men and sustained by the believing men, certain space is given to Catholic women but only as caregivers, mothers, and chaste devotees of God.*

### 3. Scriptural Subjugations: Immaculate Conception of Gender

> *"Vergine Madre, figlia del tuo figlio,"* exclaimed Dante, who perhaps best
> captures the combination of the three feminine roles — daughter-wife-mother
> (Kristeva 139)

Among others, the socialization of the human subject can be implemented
through institutionalized conceptions and dogmatic significations on gender.
As such can be evidently seen when the human subjectification is substantiated on the interplay of normative knowledge and androcentric power
structures, where the agentive individual performances of gender become
inspected, restricted or conformed to the norms of the particularities of a
religious formation. In this section, Marian conceptualizations of gender
alongside some significant examples drawn from the biblical texts are laid
out as triggering factors for the normative construction of gender roles, for
women in particular.

Virgin Mary is not only the mother of her son but she also becomes
his daughter through her faithfulness and service unto his son. In such a
mystery difficult to understand, she is also his spouse or wife; the belief
originated in the idea of Mary being pregnant with the Holy Spirit. Hence,
Kristeva argues that *"she passes through all three women's stages in the
most restricted of all possible kinship systems"* (Kristeva 139). In this sense,
I would first like to provide an overall descriptive insight into the concept
of Virgin Mary as *Mater Dei*[1] and *Co-Redemptrix*[2], and more importantly
as a gendered figure being depicted in diverse bodily colors and forms yet
remaining almost the same influential mother figure across different religious localities. I would then like to touch on what a divine female body
can constitute for the modern-day women of faith with all of her gendered
implications on body and sexuality.

For many, It is a profound expression of faith to bow before the statue
of Mary. Devotion to the male creator is performed through a humble act
of prayer to the female mother. Genuflecting before the most blessed virgin
to show gratitude and to cry out the inner pain, sorrows and yearnings
unite the believing men before a human made image of a celestial female

---

1　*'Mother of God' in Latin.*
2　*A Catholic doctrine in Mary's role in the redemption of humankind.*

divine, *the queen of heaven*. Nonetheless, the whole imagery constructed around Mary appears to be reinforcing the androcentric conceptions rather than subverting the long-existing patriarchies. The male gaze is ultimately directed beyond the female divine to its ultimate destination; *unto a male deity, Jesus*.

The presence of the male son rises above and beyond the female redemptrix, and a defenseless baby son held by the most glorious of women supersedes her under his male divinity. She is solely the *mediatrix* for man's journey to Jesus, unable to redeem, *she remains as a counterfeit figure for women's emancipation*. Although the *Redemptoris Mater*, as referred to Mary in her redemptive work in the Catholic Catechism, is not associated with teaching and leadership, she was exalted to a celestial and blessed position that she has become a key figure in the Catholic interpretation of salvation. Putting aside the theological interpretation of who she truly was, I would like to refer to the female roles of gender that she imposes on today's believing women. *The perpetual virginity of Mary* appears to be one of the key aspects in understanding the spiritual scheme that is immensely constructing the limits of gender for women, and eventually the male conception of women. Her perpetual virgin condition and immaculate conception of Jesus are two of the Marian doctrines that glorified the notion of chastity across all denominations. Not only she represents ideal believing women in her full perpetual virginity but also proposes significantly modest gender roles for the female believers in their communicative actions with the world outside. Considering how Mary has always been highly venerated within mostly the western and the eastern church, it has gradually constructed a celestial imagery of a gendered queen of heaven that ultimately has become a divine figure for all the god-fearing women of faith. Modest and obedient attitudes Mary showed, as the Bible writes, has become one of the most prominent role models for women of faith. Thus, the Marian phenomenon is still immensely relevant to today's Christian women, which is carried forward significantly through the ongoing institutional dogmatization of gender. In the contemporary world, Virgin Mary was referred as the role model for women by the Pope at the general audience. As addressed in his sermon, women were portrayed in the position of *co-operation* rather than the initiator. The affirmation of women is sought but not necessarily applied. This particular complementarian

approach to women functions not only to debunk the arguments of egalitarianism but also degrades women in her full equality to men. Therefore, the
womanhood as created by the scriptural gendered indoctrinations fosters
a broader societal and cultural scheme for women in their communicative
behaviors, nonverbal interactions, and more importantly in their intercultural dialogues.

Such gendered stigma imposed in the lives of women continues to
bleed through the adoration of a modest, meek, and obedient lifestyle.
Similarly, the imagery of the female saints along with visual and discursive representations of Mary may construe a sense of consolation and
relief to women who are oppressed by the predominantly male churches.
Marian devotion or the condition of female saints ultimately sustain the
patriarchal position of male presence by allowing the female presence in
the role of *mediators, intercessors and co-operators*. Hence, the Marian
conceptualizations on gender promises the inflicted women an illusionary
world of relief by subtly overshadowing the violation of gender equality
born out of complementarian approach to gender.

### 4. Mystification of Women

Beauvoirian argument (Beauvoir 439–638) takes us to the ancient times
where the goddesses possessed an autonomous power and acted indepen-
dently from the male presence. The ancient female deities utilized men for
their benefit and interest while Mary as a divinized female figure represents
an dependent image of women. By attributing women the roles of servant-
hood, obedience, and dependency on the male supreme, the individual
agentive role of women remains vague. Mary expresses her willingness
to be a servant with these words of obedience *"I am the Lord's servant"*[3]
admitting her inferiority before her son. It is through the obedient and
dependent imagery of the scriptural female role models that the inferior and
subjugated condition of the believing women began to rise to the surface.
Thus, divinely organized patriarchal indoctrinations become manifested
in the ordinary lives of believers. Beauvoirian argument defines women as

---

3   Luke 1:38. The Bible. Authorized King James Version, Oxford UP, 1998.

being the *"second sex"* that also refers to women's condition being defined in relation to men.

Similarly, St. Thomas saw women as the *"imperfect man,"* and the *"incidental"* being (Hauke 28). In the chapter *"Woman: Myth and Reality"* in *The Second Sex,* Beauvoir suggests that men marginalized women by the mystification of the unknown. The otherness placed on women was suggested by men who lack enough knowledge on women, and it eventually led to the dogmatic conceptions and androcentric genderization of women. Beauvoir asserted that such, in a matter of speaking, misogynistic oppression occurred not only in class and race categories but also in religious groups. Hence, it can be argued that it is significantly through gender dogmatism and standardization against women that the male predominance and patriarchal order came into a more perpetual and substantial existence (Beauvoir 21–126). Derogatory and destructive attributes placed on women originated in the creation story, where it was a woman figure who was tempted and became disobedient, are now replaced with Mary's dependent and obedient representations with the evil serpent being defeated under her feet; the serpent that once caused Eve to fall from grace. Thus, Mary is the new hope for the believing women suggesting a sense of consolation from female quilt forced by the male superiority. Though some may argue for the idea that the Marian presence contributed to the spiritual enhancement and emancipation of women in the church, the idea that she was the mother of God, a male divine son, reinforced the concepts of maternity while also making the concept of motherhood a sacred stage: *"Many civilizations have subsumed femininity under the Maternal but Christianity in its own way developed this tendency to the full"* (Kristeva 135). Thus, I argue that Mary's celestial and sublimated expression of womanhood solely appears to be a dogmatic embodiment of the female gender roles, which ultimately serve to the masculinist interests of the patriarchal church order.

## 5. Indoctrination of the Literalist Ideology on Women

The literalist approach takes the biblical doctrines exactly as they were stated in the scriptures, which I consider as forming a dichotomy for women. On the one hand, emancipation of women is appreciated but it is restrained at the level of spiritual liberation. On the other hand, the literalist indoctrination on women seems to be contributing to the androcentric objectives, which is to restrict female self-interpretations and the agentive ways of defining gender. Thus, the denied access of women to religious institutional power and clerical management is vividly evident because the Biblical portrayal of women is believed to show so. Female roles such as childbearing and nurturing are encouraged in the Bible with women being depicted as *"weaker vessels"*.[4] The male-centric order within family structuring and the religious positioning of women only on supporting roles while men to the ruling positions are some of the evident results of the literalist Christian ideology. Leadership positions and the ability to teach are attributed to men[5] while women are expected to teach in smaller groups. The Bible refers to such women as *"virtuous women"*[6] listing the valuable attributes for women to have. I do not wish to argue the truthfulness and authenticity of the Bible but it is also vitally important to mention that these dogmatic attributes form the conceptions of a biblically ideal woman. The encouraged idealization of female gender roles serves the infusion of a masculinist 'divine' power and the advancement of the hegemonic governance of the male members of the religious order, and therefore the exaltation of the masculine gender roles.

In light of the arguments above-mentioned, I would like to return to how communicational processes are affected. Our interpersonal interactions manifest our self-concept creating an area for the performance of gender roles, which is also an area for the appraisal of certain verbal and nonverbal gendered signs over other unwanted communicational marks. The idea prevailed in Judeo-Christian tradition that the evil legacy the women inherit through Eve has called forth an internalized enmity towards women due to her disobedient act against both her male company and God. The

---

4   *1.Peter 3:7 Likewise, ye husbands, dwell with them according to knowledge, giving honor unto the wife, as unto the weaker vessel, and as being heirs together of the grace of life; that your prayers be not hindered.*

5   *Ephesians 5:23 For the husband is the head of the wife, even as Christ is the head of the church: and he is the saviour of the body.*

6   *Provers 14:2 A wife of noble character is her husband's crown, but a disgraceful wife is like decay in his bones.*

consequences of such rebellion are that women were given attributes of moral inferiority and untrustworthiness. As recorded in the book of Genesis, the punishment for the disobedience of women came through labor pains, menstruation, and childbearing.

It is recorded in the bible that *"A woman should learn in quietness and full submission"*.[7] Besides, silence is considered as a virtuous act in the Bible, and it is compared to gold. However, the overemphasis of silence for women laid the groundwork for the headship roles to be taken away from women. Furthermore, it triggered the formation of hierarchical inequalities within the binary of gender. Not only the overemphasis on silence muted women vis-a-vis men but also it caused the emergence of the idealization of modesty and quietness as a desired aspect of gender for women. The Bible demonstrates the desired female gender roles as *"respectable apparel, with modesty and self-control…with braided hair and gold or pearls or costly attire"*[8] calling women to live a modest life being submissive to both their husbands and God. Thus, self-control and modesty are primarily connected to the interactional ways in which the believing women communicate with the world outside, and it ultimately forms and affects the interactional marks during cross-cultural contacts.

## 6. Biblical Manhood and Masculinity

Male representation suggesting certain gender roles such as the ones that have to do with physical strength, protection, and hunting empowered the masculinist hegemony placing men in a survival position, which then created a male-dominated religious social order. As well as for women, the biblical indoctrinations of male gender roles are equally significant. The sacred formations of gender imposed on men substantially impact on the cross-cultural interactions the believing men has with the world outside. The authoritarian essentialist nature granted to men and the supreme privileges bestowed upon the creation of men outstandingly affect the dynamics of the religious male identity. While the egalitarian approach that equalizes

---

7   1.Timothy 2:11–14. *The Bible. Authorized King James Version*, Oxford UP, 1998.

8   1.Timothy 2:9. *The Bible. Authorized King James Version*, Oxford UP, 1998.

men to women is relevant in some cases, family structures may also be predominantly built on the male dominance delegating men certain tasks that women are considered to be incapable of. Men are encouraged to stay away the futility and carnality that may mislead them to sexual impurity, and they are encouraged to abstain from the vulgar talk, unwise choices, and disloyalty.

I would like to argue that the privileges given to men may turn into a *performative burden, constrictive impositions on gender.* Considering no gendered performance is inherent to the biological body that performs the gender, men of faith are molded into the religious structuring of gender that eliminates the agentive subjectivities. With its absolute over-signification on the idealized human subject as intended by God's creation, the dreams of men remains as a pie in the sky, *an ideal man image into which all other men merge.*

A man's ultimate goal is structured around a healthy family life, a successful work life, and obedience to God. These biblical understandings of what's considered to be a godly man are also reflected on the idea that men are expected to be protective over women. Though these expectations may also concern men outside the church, it is of high importance to argue that religious doctrines, as well as the Biblical teachings on manhood and masculinity, constitute the backbone of cultural localities. Similar to women, Christian men are also affected by the clashing of distinct identities and contrasting communicational marks that occur in intercultural dialogues.

# CHAPTER FOUR    Gender and Interculturality

> *"We argue that gender is not a set of traits, nor
> a variable, nor a role, but the product of social
> doings of some sort. What then is the social doing
> of gender? It is more than the continuous creation
> of the meaning of gender through human actions.
> We claim that gender itself is constituted through
> interaction" (West et al. 127).*

Within the narrowed scope of this book and the particularity of the research unit, those who share the same religious beliefs within the same cultural locality are selected as the participants of this research. The participants are devoted believers of the Christian faith from various national backgrounds integrating into an entirely distinct cultural and religious locality, the Turkish society. I conducted qualitative semi-structured interviews with an Australian Protestant Christian Theologian and professor of the Old Testament, a German Protestant Christian pastor, and North American Protestant Christian male and female missionaries, and a Haitian Protestant Christian. All the interviews are conducted face-to-face with such questions that could direct their answers to the focus of this research.

The participants are asked to think of religious doctrines and biblical teachings as well as scriptural role models that shaped and influenced their gender roles. They are questioned on the basis of how they perform their gender in their countries of origin in comparison with their interactions with both same and opposite sex peers in their current country of residence. The interviews focus on eliciting the similarities and differences, and ultimately the contribution of their beliefs to their gender performance within an intercultural context.

The research unit consisting of cisgender participants are interviewed in their natural living settings where they are expected to restrain certain behaviors, to adopt to particularities of the local culture, or refuse to conform to the norms of the living. These interviews are conducted in the light of the ancient sacred texts that rule over the lives of the members behind the scene, and the scriptural references are provided to explain reasons behind the encouraged gender roles. The findings are eventually linked to the participant's resistance or conformity toward integration in their new area of settlement. Besides, the intersectionality between what is considered to be an effective intercultural dialogue and the performance of religious identities is shown.

In addition, primary research based on participant observations are used. For this purpose, the participating individuals were visited both in their religious communities and new environment of settlement where they seek to act on their affiliated religious identities, and thus they could naturally show how intercultural integration is encouraged or hindered based on how they believe or manage to represent their identities. Observations and analysis of the communicational behaviors of the participants who come from distinct cultural localities as well as religious identities can potentially provide significant results and contrastive perspectives on the targeted research questions of this book.

I would also like to address the prevailing cultural habitualities and the socio-cultural gendered concepts of the area of research. The involvement of Turkish women in the public sphere as a means of women's concern to publicly reflect on their femininity has long been a contested area. There has been a sense of emancipation through the unveiling of women in clothing and some other nonverbal aspects, however, the women remain unliberated as the Kemalist approach to women could not fully accomplish women's liberation in both civic spaces and public spheres. The exact same argument was made by Kandiyoti in her following words: *"Women would be refashioned as modern, equal, and active citizen-subjects. Kemalist perception of women's emancipation did not envision women's participation in the public sphere as a denial of patriarchal gender roles. In other words, women could be a part of the public sphere as sexual subjects and their primary role as mothers and house managers would remain intact"* (Kandiyoti, 1987). After all, internalized forms of hegemonic display of the androcentric dominion of men remains intact, and women have been given a social platform to a certain degree which will not violate men's public space and thus the patriarchal order.

Varying from nonverbal marks as in clothing, gestures or eye-contact to their family lives and relations with locals, the participants are willingly yet strictly dependent on the normative expectations of the religious community which they are affiliated with. As the male and female participants in Appendix A agrees, the encouraged gender roles prevalent within their religious community shape the most of their gender performance, and it also affects other dynamics such as marriage, child-rearing and family. The female obedience, for instance, suggests a male-dominated family structure that binds up women to a male-centric order. The female participant in Appendix A expressed her appreciation for how Jesus honored women, which was quite untraditional for men to do. She goes on to say that Jesus stood against the prevailing culture and treated women the way they deserve. It is important to remember that within the orthodox Judaic tradition, the social order was structured around the male presence portraying women almost inferior to men. As in almost all the expressions of the Judeo-Christian gender structuring, caregiving, nurturing, and chores were among the prominent roles allocated to women.

As discussed earlier, the authoritarian role attributed to men served the creation of a male hegemony, and it lessened the woman's involvement in many aspects of society. Therefore, it is significantly important to understand that the participants of these research are both limited in their religious communities and also in the new cultural environment they currently reside. They wish to integrate into to the new society withholding some gender expressions pertinent to their cultures of origin. For instance, the female participant in Appendix A states that the hierarchical superiority of men does not exist in her marriage and family life. As also argued by the communication accommodation theory, this leads her to *a process of divergence* and communicational clash with the local women whose gender roles are contrastively repressed under the hegemony of their male spouses.

As the male participant agrees, Christian men tend to take Jesus as a role model in a way that He was not judgmental toward women and He honored them. In this regard, I would like to refer to *Maria Magdalena*, as a role model taken by the female participants, who is one of the outstanding Biblical figures representing a sense of liberation for guilty and sinful Christian women. The oppression on the female gender was lifted off by Jesus with his unconditional act of honoring women regardless of their sinful past. Magdalena is seen as a female prostitute. For this reason, it was highly unacceptable and unlawful for religious men to even talk to her. Thus, such divine subversion of the traditional approach to women and woman's sexuality has a remarkable significance for the Christian women.

However, I argue that the same Christian men who treat women in an honoring way may also teach that women should remain in certain limitations of gender roles restricting them to enter into the masculine order. This can also be seen in the communication patterns each participant is expected to have based on their biological sex. For instance, an American Christian woman whose concept of gender is as traditional and normative as a devout Muslim women could restrain herself from interacting with local Muslim men avoiding certain nonverbal signs to prevent misconceptions on her sexuality. On the other hand, there is a considerably interesting point that stands out from the interview with the male participant in Appendix A, and it leads us to not only gender roles but also the sexuality of the participant. The male participant admits that he used to be abused by other men, acknowledging that he used to live as a gay man in his early adulthood. In his words, he justified his unwanted sexuality with an external factor of being abused. He admits that he needed to refuse his homosexual feelings if he wanted to become an obedient member of his religious community.

When the female participant in Appendix A was asked about the gender role differences between her country of origin and the host country, she mentioned the concepts of *individualism vs. collectivism*. Because she suggests that the American culture is shaped around individualism, and an individual progress is emphasized, she admits that she is challenged in her new living environment as there is a greater emphasis on the community itself. However, as alternatively seen in the integrative communication theory, the participant admits to have become more collectivist in her thinking and behaviors after a while. Coming from a society where women and men are considered to be relatively more equal, particularly outside her religious community, she feels hindered in her communication and in the expressions of her gender identity as a Christian female. The female participant can be said to have difficulty in understanding the position of so-called 'the oppressed local women' in her new cultural locality. She acknowledges that such conceptual dissimilarities lead her to a communicational chaos with both same and opposite sex. Besides, she believes that the nonverbal signs she uses through her physical appearance can be intimidating for the locals as she stands out as a blue-eyed American woman with distinctive gender marks.

The same participants argue that it is quite reasonable for both mother and father to raise the children together, and it is also appreciated when men help their wives with the housework. Though this may not be the case in more conservative Christian families where raising kids and housework are motherly tasks, it appears to me that the equal distribution of household chores is exercised among the more egalitarian Christian families. However, having moved to Turkey where there is a significant distinction of gender roles in housework and family governance, the participants are considerably challenged to the extent that they were seen as culturally disharmonious with the traditional Turkish family values by their local friends. The female participant was told that they are setting a bad example for the Turkish husbands as her husband distorts the male-centric order in the family by helping his wife with the household chores. Because caregiving and child-rearing are practiced rather differently than the common local practice, it comes as a challenge for the local to understand and even appreciate them. In the same way, the traditional role of men that is to provide for the family is equally divided in the case of the participants. All these differences that stem from distinct cultural and religious practices constitute roadblocks for the participants to effectively integrate into a new cultural locality. Similarly, their intercultural communication can be said to be immensely hindered as the divergent gender roles collide with one another. The male participant also suggests that this creates a fraction in the society as he also agrees on the idea that the interactional conflicts lead them to discomfort. Thus, the dissimilarities in gender roles do not result in the convergence of the participants but rather in the divergence from the local practice of gender roles, which also affect the dynamics of communication.

It is not only the verbal interactions but also the nonverbal signs that are equally challenged. For instance, as there are various codes of dressing among the Christian women, some women may prefer modest clothing. The overuse of jewelry is seen as seductive, and piercing the body is not appreciated among some Christian denominations. Because of the concern of being perceived as a 'loose woman,' the female participant in Appendix A dresses up differently than in the United States. It can be seen as an appropriate act for foreigners to dress in accordance with the local codes of dressing as a sign of respect but it becomes an entirely different story when it is done out of fear and anxiety of being misperceived. In this sense, I could argue that the social identity performance of the participants is inclined to a communicational divergence and avoidance over certain interactional nonverbal signs. Similarly, a public appearance with an opposite sex also worries the participants. They felt the need to make a rule that the male participant would not be alone with the female nanny of their children. Because it may not be culturally accepted for a married man to be seen with another woman, they choose to converge by compromising on their household interactions. In this regard, it is almost vital to emphasize on the idea that interactions with the opposite sex is broadly hindered and could be seen as shameful for married couples. In the local cultural context where the participants reside, for women to overly engage in conversations with the opposite sex can be seen as dishonoring. Thus, the participants are expected to adopt the interaction patterns that could be culturally appropriate for their perceived gender identity. On the other hand, the male participant in Appendix A shows us that even the peer interactions can be problematic stemming from different approach to sexuality. For instance, during one of his interactions with a same-sex local, he was offered things that he would consider sexually immoral. The constant refusal of and avoidance from such 'immoralities' led him to discomfort and anxiety in his communication with his male peers. Because the majority of men that the male participant interacts with are nominal Muslim men and that it is usually only the devoted and practicing religious Muslim men, exceptions excluded, who strictly avoid committing adultery, he admits to have been challenged not only in his dialogue with the opposite-sex but also in his same-sex interactions.

The intercultural communication often comes along with a need for social integration and interactional adaptation into the new cultural locality. The interactional challenges in cross-cultural integration arise from the long-established normativities prevailed in the hosting culture. Differences in religious practices may cause a communicational hindrance when one part is resistant to converge. The participants in Appendix A have been culturally challenged in conforming to the local religious traditions. They refuse to take part in religious ceremonies and to even accept the meat from a sacrificed animal according to Islamic tradition, which immensely affect the flow their intercultural dialogues. It is to say that because their religious conceptions restrict them, they avoid certain local religious rituals and practices that would oppose their spiritual practices. In this sense, they become cultural outcasts that disables their social integration into the deeper parts of the local lifestyle. Considering how religious structures may polarize different world-views and marginalize people of other faith, the participants believe that they are allowed to communicate with locals to the extent the locals enable them to. In societies where the religious dissimilarities are seen as a threat to effective communication, foreigners who deeply wish to integrate into the hosting society may face damaging stereotypes, misconceptions, and certain prejudice, which leads us to the vital significance of thoroughly understanding the local codes of culture for our integration into new social localities.

The indoctrination of traditional gender roles can be seen in the upbringing of the participant four as she was taught to stay home while boys could go out. Her mother was entirely dependent on her husband, and it was usually her father who made the decisions in the family. According to her words, there was such an intense father figure in the family that she disliked seeing her mother being subject to her husband. In this regard, I would like to refer to the role of the early childhood indoctrination of traditional gender roles that begin at home teaching children certain gender roles appropriate for their defined sex category. Religious communities encourage the traditional gender roles even after the children are grown up. The female participant in Appendix D made a relevant comparison between the United States and her new country of residence that she argues for women's submissive position inside a family staying the same across two cultures. She also added that it was because of her father's understanding of the Bible that he acted out a quite patriarchal figure not allowing women to partake in decision-making processes. This demonstrates the idea that the personal interpretations of the Bible may create hierarchical and male-centric family structures that can be cross-culturally challenged.

Another point worth mentioning is that the dress code is something that all the participants compromise at. As also in the case of the participant four, it is especially the women who tend to adopt into the dress code of the new environment to avoid misconceptions. The dress code is also an easy way to begin the integration process as it does not require much internal change. However, the participant four, contrary to the female participant in Appendix A, seems to be converging more by wearing only long skirts and leaving her jeans away. It is mostly the traditional older women who would dress long skirts in Turkey, and it can be a symbol of modesty as well as a sign for belonging to a certain type of living. In her case, long skirts are used as a nonverbal mark representing her modest and religious lifestyle. Because it is not seductive or charming by any means, she believes that she avoids unwanted contact with the opposite-sex. By overly simplifying herself, she reduces her communicational anxiety and stays away from contact with men that help her integrate more effectively, although as such may be considered an authentic integration. However, based on my observations, it is also crucial to mention that she was not much welcomed into the non-religious or nominal parts of the city as the locals considered her quite pious and bizarre. As a result, she represents her faith by certain nonverbal expressions of clothing and by modest use of bodily gestures that ultimately create her way of gender and thus the performance of her femininity.

Concerning her intercultural contact with locals, she prefers to avoid eye-contact and touching. Thus, the application of the proxemics and haptic can be argued to be quite different from how they would be practiced in the United States as the avoidance of them is higher in Turkey. Unless they are Christian men. she admits that she does not talk to men at all. Objectifying men as a sexual threat to her sexuality removes all the possibilities for her to interact with the opposite-sex. Considering her own words *'I wear skirts because this is who I am,'* she identifies herself with the merits and religious significations of wearing a skirt, which she considers to be for someone who is piously modest. Considering that Islam also praises chastity for women, the participant's performance of her sexuality is not challenged in Turkey, as she resembles herself to Turkish women. She further says that because of her religious background that constitutes the strongest part of her identity, she found it significantly easier to integrate into the new cultural environment. However, because of her Christian values that view non-believer men almost as a sexual threat to God-fearing women, her gender performance remains 'unstained and secluded' from the carnalities of the world outside.

The female participant in Appendix B admits that the writings of the Apostle Paul immensely shaped her gender roles and that she prefers to maintain a modest life in all aspects. Thus, it is essential to understand the connection between how the concept of modesty affects the nonverbal man-ners through which they communicate and how it shapes the ways in which they perform their gender on cross-cultural grounds. The idea that women should behave and live modestly impacts on the interaction patterns, and it forms certain verbal and nonverbal signs that comply with the intended impression. The use of body, gestures, dress code, intonation, and vocabu-lary are some of the things that are affected by the observance of modesty. As the female participant also stated, women's ability to teach remains controversial among the Christian denominations. Though the term mod-esty has a positive connotation, it fundamentally affects woman's unequal positioning vis-à-vis men and reinforces the male-dominated structures. As she also agrees, the performance of gender for the believing woman is highly dependent on the Biblical teachings on gender roles. Hence, it is significantly important to consider the sacred texts when studying the relationship between intercultural communication and social identities. The male participant in Appendix B suggests that he no longer sees women as a sexual taboo and treats women with utter respect. He also claims to have been influenced by complementarian approach to gender roles and admits that society tends to position men superior to women. Because there is an encouraged complementarian order within the family structure of Christians while the local family structuring in the hosting Islamic context is predominantly dependent on the male presence, his concept of fatherhood and being a husband vis-à-vis the local understanding is confronted with certain conflicts: 'When I talk to guys, if I lived in Istanbul for example where people sleep around, they expect me I would have also slept around. When I told them I never slept around, I stayed a virgin till I was married, a big shock. For a lot of young Turkish guys, they are supposed to exper-iment it'.

More interestingly, all of the male participants avoid even the same-sex peer interactions at a certain level, and their contact with the local men are therefore not intimate. Because there is a direct connection between who we communicate and our identities we perform, the male participants prefer to have deeper dialogues with like-minded peers of the same faith while the locals are approached to and interacted with to a certain level. In this sense, it can be argued that the exclusive nature of religion encourages the participant believers to stay away from the world outside while, quite contrastingly, they dream of becoming a local-like.

Besides the changes in verbal interactions, there is also an avoidance of certain nonverbal behaviors. The female participant in Appendix B would smile more and have more eye-contact in the United States but she avoids all these nonverbal signs in Turkey as she sees them a threat to her religious gender identity. She also avoids hand-shaking with men and does not look in the eyes directly. Because the participants are overtly confident in their religious identities that affect the way they interact, *the avoidance of these nonverbal behaviors becomes a means to perform their religious gender identity demonstrating the locals their dissimilar identity marks and exclusionary interactional manners.* In this sense, the intercultural communication takes place not only between people of different cultures but also between people who represent themselves ideologically and ethically distinct from the locals. *The communicational efficiency is no longer the matter; the ultimate concern is then to both maintain and represent the religious identity through avoidance and reductionist mechanisms in the performance of gender.* The avoidance occurs when the conversation is not matching with the participant's identity performance, and thus he may prefer to alter the dialogue based on his religious interests: *"They talked about girls in a degrading way. That is the sort of conversation that I do not like. It happens with young guys, and I try to change the conversation quickly."*

I would like to address to one of the local cultural conceptions around the elderly people that it is considered inappropriate to teach an older man or to show a level of knowledge that surpasses theirs. The male participant cannot initiate conversation with older men as he finds it difficult to engage in interaction with elderly people. The communication is rather non-reciprocal when interacting with elderly people as his interactional assertiveness could be considered as disrespectful. Though the Bible also encourages to respect the elders, the Islamic or oriental understanding relatively differently encourages the younger men to respectfully and fearfully approach elderly people, which the male participants find challenging. Consequently, as the participants in Appendix B would agree, the possible misconceptions that the locals may have on them and the fear or anxiety of being misunderstood largely affect the participants' performance of gender. For instance, the female participant expressed her constant fear of being misperceived with her following statement *"I feel like the perception of male here when they see a foreigner female, they would think I am easy to sleep with"* and that *"It has taken time for me to learn modesty in this culture, in a way that I feel comfortable and I can be perceived as someone who loves God"*. As a result, she found her way to make herself comfortable by changing her nonverbal interactions and dress code through which she represents a 'Godly woman' to the local environment.

## 1. Convergence Through Self-Struggle

*"Femininity is imposed for the most part through an unremitting discipline that concerns every part of the body and is continuously recalled through the constraints of clothing or hairstyle."* (Bourdieu 23)

I am interested in the pressurizing effects the biblical characters may have on both the intersubjective and intercultural contact of believers. Considering how the dogmatic embodiments of gender roles may take away the individual agency on gender, *I argue that the antiquity itself has significant potentialities in creating particular attributions and behavioral patterns as role models for the believer to adopt so that they may be considered righteous and decent members both within and outside their religious communities.* For instance, the participant seven was often compared to Esther and Mary in the Bible, and she was expected to behave appropriately and do things that are rightful to the role model she represents. However, she felt oppressed and constrained to a level where there was no room left for her to make mistakes. Consequently, she had to conceal many aspects of her life that eventually led her to sustain a life of dishonesty and less integrity: *"I was fighting with myself. I knew I had to be the certain way, not because I wanted it but because of people who had expectations on me. Everybody believed in me. I was fighting with myself. Because I did not want to disappoint them."*

Not only she had interactional issues within her religious community but she was also restrained from integrating into the world outside the church.

She was not allowed to talk to the opposite-sex and was not permitted to have an emotional relationship with men. Moreover, she admits that her gender was entirely shaped and influenced by the religious community she was born into. After all, she ended up moving to Turkey where she had her first ear piercing and that she found herself in a wholly distinct culture as a woman whose gender has always been under an institutional control. Because she was taught to abstain from the opposite-sex relationships and was forcefully encouraged to dress modestly, it was an absolute intercultural challenge for her to integrate into the new locality. In her religious culture, religious women were expected to wear skirts, and jeans were not appropriate for women. For this reason, she kept wearing skirts in Turkey, where she moved for her self-freedom, but the locals were staring at her as though she was naked. Thus, her previous gender mark of her modest dress code was significantly challenged in Turkey where she ended up starting wearing jeans. In doing so, she avoided the possible misperceptions by converging into the new cultural locality. More outstandingly is that she ended up giving up on the religious gender roles she grew up with and decided to separate her female gender representation from her religious beliefs. As such stands out to be a remarkable case of cultural convergence into the local ways of living. She further explains some of her interactional challenges with the case of the kind of food she cooked being refused by the locals for the idea that she is Christian, which they thought makes her food 'unclean'. Her intention in cooking for the locals was to show the feminine hospitality she learned growing up in her local church. Another example is that she was often confused with prostitutes and was offered to have sex for money. This was an absolute threat to her sense of Christian morality, which ultimately led her to feel constant anxiety hindering the efficiency of her intercultural integration.

## 2. Biblical Gender Roles Through a Feminist Theologian

I would like to begin this section with the remarks of the participant six in Appendix F who is a well-known theologian within the Protestant denomination and a Biblical scholar of the Old Testament. Contrary to the other female participants, she supports the egalitarianism in gender roles, discards the submissive roles of women, and believes in the right for women to become teachers and leaders. She explains the way in which she conceptualizes the gender binary and the biblical gender roles quite openly: *"For a woman to look up to as role models within the Biblical texts are particularly the ones in the Old Testament such as Deborah in the Book of Judges. She was a judge, prophet, and leader to Israel. Even Esther capitulated the culture in her time. She was courageous, and her decisions were brave which is very inspirational. There are also women in the New Testament particularly in the Book of Acts like Priscilla. Also, Lydia who was a leader in the early church. These women were teachers and were very instrumental in the establishment of the early church."* The female prophets that influenced the course of the Biblical history affect the gender roles of the modern-day believer in a way that the women find comfort, strength, and right to be influential and to take the initiative.

On the other hand, there are apparent differences in her communication style as she performs her interactions majorly considering her religious identity. For instance, she avoids hand shaking and certain dialogues with men that did not matter at all back in Australia. Her perception on the local conception of how women should behave and interact also affected her communicational approach as she states that *"I am not quite sure what to do. I tend to hesitate, and I wait to respond. I have taken a very passive role whereas in Australia I would be much more active in being an initiator in conversations or interactions. I am not an initiator here."* Because she thinks that the local women tend to communicate much more passively than the local men, she expresses her concerns over her restricted gender performance by saying *"I do not want to offend people and be culturally insensitive which leads to hesitancy, and that is also a hindrance."*

Besides, she avoids the implications that her social identities could impose on her. Thus, she abstains from interactional signs that could mark her as a Christian Western woman. She explains such abstention as *"I am much more aware of being conservative in clothing trying not to be obviously western. Because that draws negative attention."* Contrary to the other female participants who find it inappropriate to approach men, she encounters people of both genders and finds it easy to contact both men and women. Nonetheless, she finds herself in an interactional conflict: *"I had some interactions with an Imam so he would say that I was a woman with lower status. I was told that my interactions should be with women, so very much division of genders."*

As previously also mentioned by other participants, the participant three in Appendix C also supports the idea that there is a male-dominated family structure in the Islamic countries that goes against his male gender roles within his family as a Christian man. The participant three sees Jesus as his role model who encourages the traditional male gender roles such as providing and caring. However, the example that the participant sees in his role model leads him to support his wife for housework that he considers as opposing to the traditional Islamic role of men in the family. On the other hand, the participant three is majorly affected by the locals who keep distance towards the foreigners by avoiding close contact with him. As he also would agree, this negatively affects his integration process into his new cultural locality hindering him being more adapted to local ways of living. As he states that *"The question is how much do I let myself be affected,"* the participant adopted some parts of the culture that he considers as the positive aspects of the local culture. However, he is concerned when the locals force him to do things that he does not agree with. Examples of it are the local traditions such as animal sacrifice or henna night that go against his religious beliefs. At this point, his religious identity collides with the local expectations on him. He also feels challenged by the local understanding of dress code as he thinks it should align with the person's professional role in the society. However, as a male religious leader, he prefers to wear quite modestly and casually. The local perception of religious dress code, however, suggests an entirely different visual concept that hinders him from representing himself with his religious identity. On the other hand, he suggests that it was particularly the Christianity that shaped the German culture, where he considers people to be more valued as individuals. He does not necessarily think that his social identities are appreciated by the locals, and that his performance of gender roles based on his Christian values are challenged and disregarded by the local environment.

# CHAPTER FIVE  Dogmatization of Subjective Identities

While the scheme of dogma constitutes the definite basis on which the communicational signifiers are conceived, the violated signified image of identity gives way to emotional upheavals and interactional discomfort. Eventually, inefficient representations of identity may lead to a performative failure, potentially resulting in integration ambiguities. As a consequence, the participants are faced with difficulties in finding ways to perform their desired gender roles vis-à-vis the local normativities. There are various scriptural figures and biblical role models that are the dogmatic source for the performance of gender roles. Varying from the representations of the Virgin Mary to Mary Magdalene, individuals whose religious identity significantly affects the other aspects of their social presence tend to take these biblical figures as role models to be the constructive basis for their gender.

Scriptural figures including David, Moses, Martha and Mary, Deborah, and Esther suggest contemporary definitions of ancient presuppositions on gender roles while encouraging the believers to interact in line with these pre-defined gendered conventionalities. Considering the fluidity and the evolving condition of cultures, intercultural dialogues become a performative stage whereby the desired impressions of identity are enforced upon the cultural other. In this sense, cross-cultural contact is limited to the extent in which an embodied ideology in the form of a human is effectively represented. Thus, the symbolic occurrences and representational normativities on the performance of gender play a remarkable role in the implementation of cross-cultural interactions in a way that the hegemonic ideologies imposed on religious identities have the potential to dictate, inspect, and re-construct the communication patterns for a cyclic reproduction of its dogmatic structuring.

Intercultural communication is an area of contestation over social identities affected by how different cultural localities define and perform gender roles. Although these social identities are performed through certain verbal and nonverbal markers, their effectiveness relies on a common understanding of their interpreted meaning. Thus, the performance of social identities can lead to misunderstandings stemming from the misinterpretations of the identity markers. Within the binary structuring of gender, women are subject to the cultural impositions of traditional gender roles around the globe. While some resist and challenge these dogmatic roles, others accept and embrace them as a part of their devotion to God. The intercultural integration of the participants of this book is affected in various ways depending on the representational and performative social identity mark. The female participants who are devoted to observe the rules of their faith and conform to the expectations of the traditional gender roles have difficulties in their interactions with the opposite sex and how the opposite sex conceives them. Their preferred communication suggests specific verbal and nonverbal codes that foster and sustain their social identities, and thus communication becomes an area of not a bidirectional process in which a message is conveyed between two recipients but rather a process in which identities are represented as a means of divergence or detachment from the local culture.

It is for this reason that there is hardly any integrative process into the new cultural environment with the divergent behaviors of the participants resulting in significant roadblocks for social and cultural integration. The female participants have challenges in arranging their dress code, gestures, eye contact, and distance with the locals, and their resistant effort to maintain their distance with the locals arise from their religious identity that eliminates interactions with locals, the opposite-sex in particular. They tend to have high self-esteem and feel secure in their own communities, and they are constrained from the many forms of the local social life. The female participants have difficulty in communicating with other local women simply because there are gendered limitations and dogmatically coded definitions on their gender performances that vary from the local aspects. Their femininity is relatively conserved because the men are seen as 'human predators,' resulting in significant levels of detachment from all sorts of communicative dialogues with their local contacts. The female participants tend to abstain from locations and situations that are not encouraged by their ideal gender roles. Most of them prefer to live in the limited structure of their families and religious communities.

Varying from socio-religious representations and interactional patterns to dress code and other nonverbal signs, the participants are hindered in their social integration to avoid misconceptions that the locals may have on their identities. It should also be noted although most of the participants come from a western country; it does not seem to have much influence on their lifestyle because their religious identities mostly override their national identities. Cultural norms are formed through the active involvement of various factors, one of which is the religious indoctrinations on the construction of cultures, which eventually serve the formation of culture-specific interactional patterns. It is to say that it is often through the unequal distribution of the dogmatic power on gender, the normative roles are readily defined for people to adopt. Such structural order brings about pre-defined behaviors of interaction through which intercultural contact is shaped, and gender roles are performed. Thus, knowledge is constituted by the layers of power, and it maintains, dictates, and preserves certain behavioral and communicational norms within the androcentric hierarchical order of power distribution. As a consequence, it stands out that both the continuation and preservation of traditional gender roles limit diversity and freedom of expression. While the religious dogmas attempt to dictate essentialist gender roles that undermine the social and cultural processes in which gender is constructed, it is the same dogmas that have been subject to a method of historical construction where social and cultural elements were the constitutive factors of its own dogma.

Above all, I have sought to bring your diligent consideration for the acknowledgment of the gendered stigma emerging through the institutionalized androcentrism that is structured from within scriptural texts, biblical figures, and phallocentric indoctrinations on the condition of women.

# REFERENCES

## Books & Journals

Adler, Peter S. "The Transitional Experience: an Alternative View of Culture Shock." Sage Journals, vol. 15, no. 4, 1 Oct. 1975. pp. 13–23.

Anderson, R., & Ross, V. Questions of communication: A practical introduction to theory (2nd ed.). New York: St. Martin's Press. 1998. pp. 20–50.

Arweck, E. & Nesbitt, E. Young people's identity formation in mixed-faith families: continuity or discontinuity of religious traditions? Journal of Contemporary Religion, 25. 2010. pp. 67–87.

Ausubel, David P. "Acculturative Stress in Modern Maori Adolescence". *Child Development*. 31. 1960. pp. (4): 617–631.

Berger, C. & Calabrese, R. "Some Explorations in Initial Interaction and Beyond: Toward a Developmental Theory of Interpersonal Communication." Human Communication Research. 1975. pp. 99–112.

Beauvoir, Simone de. "Woman: Myth and Reality". in Jacobus, Lee A. (ed.). *A World of Ideas*. Bedford/St. Martins, Boston 2006. pp. 21–126.

Beauvoir, Simone de. "Woman: Myth and Reality". in Jacobus, Lee A. (ed.). *A World of Ideas*. Bedford/St. Martins, Boston 2006. pp. 780–795.

Bourdieu, P. Distinction: A Social Critique of the Judgement of Taste. London: Routledge. 1984.

Bourdieu, Pierre, and Richard Nice. Outline of a Theory of Practice. 1977. p.155.

Bourdieu, Pierre, and Richard Nice. Masculine Domination. 2001. p. 23.

Burgoon, J.K.; Hale, J.L. "Nonverbal Expectancy Violations: Model Elaboration and Application to Immediacy Behaviors". *Communication Monographs*. 1988. pp. 58–79.

Butler, Judith. "Performative Acts and Gender Constitution: An Essay in Phenomenology and Feminist Theory," *Theatre Journal* 40, no. 4. 1988. pp. 519–531.

Butler, Judith. "Imitation and Gender Insubordination1." Cultural theory and popular culture: A reader 1. 2006. pp. 255.

Butler, Judith. Bodies That Matter: On the Discursive Limits of "Sex". New York: Routledge.1993. p. 95.

Cragan, J. F., & Shields, D.C. Understanding communication theory: The communicative forces for human action. Boston, MA: Allyn & Bacon. 1998. pp. 274–276.

Deleuze, Gilles, and Fĺix Guattari. Anti-oedipus: Capitalism and Schizophrenia. London: Continuum, 2003.

Foucault, Michel. The History of Sexuality. New York: Pantheon Books, 1978. pp. 1–133.

Foucault M. The subject and power. Afterword by Michel Foucault. In: Dreyfus HL, Rabinow P, editors. Beyond structuralism and hermeneutics. New York: Harvester Wheatsheaf; 1982. pp. 208–226.

Foucault, Michel. The Order of Things: An Archaeology of the Human Sciences. New York: Vintage Books, 1994. pp. 375–380.

Gallois, Cynthia; Callan, Victor J. "Interethnic Accommodation: The Role of Norms." In Giles, Howard; Coupland, Justine; Coupland, N. Contexts of Accommodation. New York: Cambridge University Press. 1991. pp. 245–269.

Giles, Howard; Smith, Philip. "Accommodation Theory: Optimal Levels of Convergence." In Giles, Howard; St. Clair, Robert N. Language, and Social Psychology. Baltimore: Basil Blackwell. 1979. pp. 45–65.

Giles, Howard; Coupland, Joustine; Coupland, N. "Accommodation Theory: Communication, Context, and Consequence." In Giles, Howard; Coupland, Justine; Coupland, N. Contexts of Accommodation. New York, NY: Cambridge University Press. 1991. pp. 1–68.

Giles, Howard; Ogay, Tania. "Communication Accommodation Theory." In Whaley, Bryan B.; Samter, Wendy. Explaining Communication: Contemporary Theories and Exemplars. Mahwah, NJ: Lawrence Erlbaum. 2007. pp. 293.

Goffman, Erving. The Presentation of Self in Everyday Life. New York: Doubleday. 1959. pp. 132–152.

Grant, Robert M. Gods and the One God. Philadelphia: Westminster Press. 1986. pp. 1–20.

Greenfield, E.A., & Marks, N.F. Religious, social identity as an explanatory factor for associations between more frequent formal religious participation and psychological well-being. International Journal for the Psychology of Religion. 2007. pp. 245–259.

Griffin, Em. "Anxiety/Uncertainty Management Theory of William Gudykunst." A First Look at Communication Theory. McGraw-Hill, n.d. pp. 426–38.

Griffin, Em. "Chapter 7: Expectancy Violations Theory". *A First Look at Communication Theory* (8 ed.). The McGraw-Hill Companies, Inc. 2012. pp. 84–92.

Gudykunst, W. B. Cross-cultural and intercultural communication. Thousand Oaks: Sage. 2003. pp. 1–53.

Gudykunst, W. B. Theorizing about intercultural communication. Thousand Oaks, Calif. Sage. 2005. Print. pp. 3–25.

Gudykunst, B. William. Understanding Must Precede Criticism: A Response to Yoshitake's Critique of Anxiety/Uncertainty Management Theory, *Intercultural Communication Studies* XII. 2003. pp. 1–28.

Gudykunst, B. William. An anxiety/uncertainty management (AUM) theory of effective communication: Making the mesh of the net finer, in W. B. Gudykunst, ed., *Theorizing about Intercultural Communication*. Thousand Oaks, CA: SAGE. 2005. p. 282.

Gudykunst, B. Willaim. An anxiety/uncertainty management (AUM) theory of effective communication: Making the mesh of the net finer, in W. B. Gudykunst, ed., *Theorizing about Intercultural Communication*. Thousand Oaks, CA: SAGE. 2005. p. 285.

Gudykunst, B. William. *Bridging Differences: Effective Intergroup Communication*. Thousand Oaks, CA: SAGE 2004. p. 130.

Gudykunst, B. William. An anxiety/uncertainty management (AUM) theory of effective communication: Making the mesh of the net finer, in W. B. Gudykunst, ed., *Theorizing about Intercultural Communication*. Thousand Oaks, CA: SAGE 2005. p. 298.

Gudykunst, B. William. *Bridging Differences: Effective Intergroup Communication*. Thousand Oaks, CA: SAGE. 2004. pp. 255–256.

Gudykunst, B. William. An anxiety/uncertainty management (AUM) theory of effective communication: Making the mesh of the net finer, in W. B. Gudykunst, ed., *Theorizing about Intercultural Communication*. Thousand Oaks, CA: SAGE. 2005. pp. 302–303.

Gudykunst, W.B. & Hammer, M.R. Strangers and hosts: An uncertainty reduction based theory of intercultural adaptation. In Y.Y. Kim and W.B Gudykunst (Eds.) Cross-Cultural adaptation: Current Approaches. Newbury Park, CA: Sage. 1988. pp. 106–139

Hauke, Manfred. God Or Goddess?: Feminist Theology: What is it?: Where Does it Lead?. Ignatius Press. 1995. p. 28.

Hecht, M. L., Collier, M. J., & Ribeau, S. A. *African American communication: Ethnic identity and cultural interpretation.* Newbury Park, CA: Sage. 1993. pp. 199–235.

Horsley, Richard. Bandits, Prophets, and Messiahs: Popular Movements in the Time of Jesus. San Francisco: Harper & Row. 1988. pp. 1–48.

Hofstede, Geert, 'Levels of Culture' in Hofstede, G., *Cultures and Organizations. Software of the Mind.* Harper Collins. 1991. p. 10.

Hofstede, Geert. Masculinity and Femininity: The Taboo Dimension of National Cultures. Sage Publications. International Educational and Professional Publisher, Thousand Oaks. 1998. pp. 77–102.

Hofstede, G. Culture's consequences. Beverly Hills, CA: Sage Publications. 1980. pp. 13–211.

Johnson, Joy; Repta, Robin. "Sex and Gender: Beyond the Binaries". *Designing and conducting gender, sex, & health research.* 2002. pp. 17–39.

Kandiyoti, Deniz. (2003). "The Paradoxes of Masculinity: Some Thought on Segregated Societies." Dislocating Masculinity: Comparative Ethnographies, by Andrea Cornwall and Nancy Lindisfarne, Routledge, p. 209.

Katz, J. The invention of heterosexuality. New York: Dutton. 1995. pp. 33–83.

Kelly, Dorothy. Reconstructing Woman: From Fiction to Reality in the Nineteenth-Century French Novel. Penn State University Press, 2007. p. 3. JSTOR, www.jstor.org/stable/10.5325/j.ctt7v302. Accessed 13 Sept. 2021.

Kim, Young Yun. Becoming Intercultural: An Integrative Theory of Communication and Cross-Cultural Adaptation. Thousand Oaks, CA: Sage. 2001. pp. 3–10.

Kim, Young Yun. "From Ethnic to Interethnic: The Case for Identity Adaptation and Transformation." Journal of Language and Social Psychology 25. 2006. 3: pp. 283–300.

Kim, Young Yun. Communication and Cross-cultural Adaptation: An Integrative Theory. Clevedon, United Kingdom: Multilingual Matters. 1988. pp. 15–40.

Kim, Young Yun. Toward an interactive theory of communication-acculturation. In B. Ruben (Ed.), Communication Yearbook 3. 1979. pp. 435–453.

Kim, Young Yun. Communication patterns of foreign immigrants in the process of acculturation. Human Communication Research. 4. 1977. pp. 66–77.

King, V. Elder, G.H., Whitbeck, L.B. Religious involvement among rural youth: An ecological and life-course perspective. Journal of Research on Adolescence, 7. 1997. pp. 431–456.

King, P.E. & Boyatzis, C.J. Exploring adolescent spiritual and religious development: current and future theoretical and empirical perspectives. Applied Developmental Science 8. 2010. pp. 2–6.

Kristeva, Julia, and Arthur Goldhammer. "Stabat Mater." Poetics Today, vol. 6, no. 1/2, 1985, pp. 133–152.

Becket J., Z. Milan. London, Routledge.p. 316.

Langer, Ellen. Mindfulness. Reading, MA: Addison-Wesley 1989. pp. 62.

Lee, C.M. & Gudykunst, W.B. Attraction in initial interethnic interactions. New Brunswick: Transaction Periodicals. Consortium. 1977. pp. 373–387..

Lee, J.J. Religion and college attendance: Change among students. The Review of Higher Education, 25. 2002. pp. 369–384.

Levine, Jill, Amy., & Maria, Mayo, Robbins. A feminist companion to Mariology. 2005. p. 147

Littlejohn, Stephen W., and Karen A. Foss. Encyclopedia of Communication. 1st ed. Vol. 1. Sage Publications, 2009. pp. 248–50.

L'Osservatore Romano. Weekly Edition in English. 13 December 1995. p. 11.

Lueck & Wilson (2011). "Acculturative stress in Latino immigrants: The impact of social, socio-psychological and migration-related factors.". International Journal of Intercultural Relations. 2011. pp. 35: 186–195.

Massey, Doreen. "Introduction: Geography Matters." In *Geography Matters! A Reader*, eds. Doreen Massey and John Allen. Cambridge: Cambridge UP, 1984, 1–12

Houser, M. L. "Are We Violating Their Expectations? Instructor Communication Expectations of Traditional and Nontraditional Students". *Communication Quarterly*. Taylor & Francis Online. 2005. 53 (2): pp. 217–218.

Pope Paul VI, Encyclical Epistle Christi Matri (15 September 1966): AAS 58. 1966. pp. 745–749

Prosser, Michael H. The Cultural Dialogue: An Introduction to Intercultural Communication. SIETER International. 1985. pp. 10–344.

Raven, Bertram H. "Kurt Lewin Address: Influence, Power, Religion, and the Mechanisms of Social Control." Wiley Online Library. Journal of Social Issues 55.1 (1999): pp. 161–86.

Sam, David L.; Berry, John W. "Acculturation When Individuals and Groups of Different Cultural Backgrounds Meet". *Perspectives on Psychological Science*. 5. 2010. pp. (4): 472.

Schwartz, S. H. Mapping and interpreting cultural differences around the world. In H. Vinken, J. Soeters, & P Ester (Eds.), *Comparing cultures, Dimensions of culture in a comparative perspective*. Leiden, The Netherlands: Brill. 2004. pp. 43–73.

Simmel, Georg. The Stranger. The Sociology of Georg Simmel. New York: Free Press. 1976. pp. 8–34.

Spitzberg, H. Brian. A model of intercultural communication competence, in L. Samovar & R. Porter, ed., *Intercultural Communication: A Reader*, 2nd ed. Belmont, CA: Wadsworth. 2000. pp. 7–24.

Stagg, Evelyn and Frank. *Woman in the World of Jesus*. Philadelphia: Westminster Press, 1978. pp. 101–110.

Tavard H. George. *The thousand faces of the Virgin Mary*. 1996. p. 253

Tajfel. H. The social categorization. In S. Moscovia (Ed.). *Introduction to Social Psychology*. Vol. 1. 1972. pp. 272–302.

Tajfel, H., & Turner, J. C. An integrative theory of intergroup conflict. *The social psychology of intergroup relations*. 1979. pp. 33–47.

The Bible. Authorized King James Version, Oxford UP, 1998.

Turner, Lynn H.; West, Richard. "Communication Accommodation Theory". *Introducing Communication Theory: Analysis and Application* (4th ed.). New York, NY: McGraw-Hill. 2010. p. 492.

Zhou, Min. "Segmented Assimilation: Issues, Controversies, and Recent Research on the New Second Generation". *International Migration Review*. 31. 1997. pp. (4): 975–1008.

Wacquant, L. (2005). Habitus. International Encyclopedia of Economic Sociology.

West, C. & Zimmerman, D. H. "Doing gender". *Gender and Society*. 1987. 1 (2): 125–151; p. 127

Williams, George Hunston. *The Radical Reformation* Philadelphia: Westminster Press, 1962. p. 430.

Wolff, H. Kurt. *The Sociology of Georg Simmel.* New York: The Free Press. 1950. pp. 402–408.

Xu, Jun. "Brief Analysis on Cross-cultural Communication." Theory and Practice in Language Studies. Academy Publication. 2011. pp. 884–87.

## Online Sources

Bridges, William, and Susan Mitchell. "Leading Transition: A New Model for Change by William Bridges and Susan Mitchell." pp. 1–8. Accessed 10 September 2017. www.crowe-associates.co.uk.

Catholic Church. *Catechism of the Catholic Church.* Vatican City: Libreria Editrice Vaticana. 2012. Accessed 25 August 2017.

"Cultural Adaptation Models." AFS Digital Intercultural Learning, AFS Intercultural Programs. Accessed 30 August 2017. icllibrary.afs.org/cms/index.php/en/.

Davidson, Deborah. Class Lecture. Introduction to Women's Studies. Wilfrid Laurier University, Waterloo. 21 Jan 2009. Accessed 15 September 2017. https://ualberta.academia.edu/DabraDavidson/CurriculumVitae

Kim, Young Yun. Development of intercultural identity. Paper presented at the annual conference of the International Communication Association, Miami FLA. 1992. Accessed 5 September 2017. http://www.wichert.org/icid.html

McLeod, S. A. Social Identity Theory. 2008. Accessed 15 July 2017. www.simplypsychology.org/social-identity-theory.html

Oberg, Kalervo.1954. "Culture Shock". Panel discussion at the Midwest regional meeting of the Institute of International Education in Chicago, November 28, 1951. Accessed 12 July 2017. http://www.smcm.edu/Academics/internationaled/Pdf/cultureshockarticle.pdf.

Robinson, B. A. "Ontario Consultants on Religious Tolerance." Religious Tolerance. N.p. 31 Jan. 2016. Web. Accessed 28 March 2017. http://www.religioustolerance.org.

Saint Ambrose, Expos. Evang. sec. Lucam, II, 7: CSEL 32/4, 45; De Institutione Virginis, XIV, 88–89: PL 16, 341. Accessed 25 September 2017. https://w2.vatican.va/content/john-paul-ii/en/encyclicals/documents/hf_jp-ii_enc_25031987_redemptoris-mater.pdf

Saleem, Amjad. "Religious Identity and Inclusion." State of Formation. Accessed 10 August 2017. www.stateofformation.org/2016/08/religious-identity-and-inclusion/.

Shaffer, M., & Reeves, J. A. "Foreigners in their own country." *The Arizona Republic. 2003.* Accessed 5 September 2017. http://www.azcentral.com/news/articles/0928polyg-males28.html

Wright, N.T. "Women's Service in the Church: The Biblical Basis". 2004. Accessed 10 September 2017. http://ntwrightpage.com/2016/07/12/womens-service-in-the-church-the-biblical-basis/

Yip, George. "A Theoretical Basis of Intercultural Communication Competence: Gudykunst's Anxiety/Uncertainty Management Theory." Global Missiology English 2.7. 2010. Accessed 15 September 2017. http://ojs.globalmissiology.org/index.php/english/

# APPENDICES

## Appendix A - American Christian Missionaries

### Participants 1 (Male & Female Interviewees)

**Participant Background:** Participants in this interview are a married missionary couple living in Turkey. The female participant graduated from the Oklahoma State University with a master's degree in nutrition specializing in education. Her husband graduated from the Oklahoma State University majoring in consultancy and holds a master's degree in divinity. He worked as a development coordinator and lecturer at the Oklahoma State University. He worked as the former Pastor/Coordinator of College/ Young Adult Ministries at First Baptist Church of Vacaville. He is also the author of the book titled 'The Hospitality of God.' Together with his wife and two children, he lives in Turkey as active member of a local religious community ministering to the needs of the church and reaching out to Muslim population with the message of the Bible. They send their children to a local state school with an aim to develop friendships with locals.

### The Interview Transcription

| | |
|---|---|
| Interviewer: | Can you think of examples of religious deities and figures in your religious culture which influenced your gender role and performance? (For instance, life of David or Jesus for men/ Mary and other biblical women figures) |
| Female participant: | I think what influenced me the most had to be the culture of the church and the denomination I grew up in. It was Baptist. They had certain ideas of what women roles are and what marriage should look like. The man is the head and the woman is inferior to man. So, for me growing up this was what I was taught but not necessarily what I experience in my house. |
| Interviewer: | Did you relate yourself to any of the biblical figures? |

| | |
|---|---|
| Female participant: | I think Mary Magdalene who was at the feet of Jesus washing his feet with her hair and He delivered her from demons and set her free. It was at that time was anti-culture because in the biblical time it was very untraditional for a man to do something for women. So I like how he treats her and honors her. I relate myself to her in this way because He has done the same for me in my life. He also honored her in front of others which was very anti-culture. |
| Interviewer: | What about you? (Referring to the male participant) |
| Male participant: | I did not become a Christian till I was twenty so I did not grow up in a Christian home. However, I believed there was a God. In my mind, God was a man. Jesus referred to God as a father, so there is some male aspect to God. However, the Bible says that God is a spirit. There is a book titled The Shack which refers to God as a woman. Many people think it is heresy. Early on as a Christian, I was thought to be more like Jesus. I do not think that I have ever looked at a role model other than Jesus, but my perception of who Jesus is was shaped by the culture I lived in. It was very conservative and political Christian culture. Today, I do try to look at Jesus as a role model because He did not judge people but rather always honored them. |
| Interviewer: | We all are attributed to certain codes of masculinity and femininity. Because you were born as a man, the Bible attributes certain gender roles to you. Do you adapt or absorb masculine features from Jesus? |
| Male participant: | Not really. Because I lived such a non-christian life for twenty years, to be a man was to conquer a woman. I do not think I thought it that way but it was the way I lived it out. I was a drug-dealer, and I was sexually abused by some men, and so I think part of my early young adult life was maybe proving that I was gay. Not that I felt gay, but because of the things that happened to me, I wanted to make sure that was clear. |
| Interviewer: | So we can say that you were in a clash between your lately obtained Christian faith which defined you in certain gender limitations and your life before you became Christian which was distinct to your current gender performance. |
| Male participant: | Today I also believe that there are defined certain roles which I draw from my understanding of my faith. |
| Interviewer: | Think about the way you perform your gender in your country of origin (how you lived as a woman) and compare it to other women here in your current country of residence. What are the differences and similarities? Above all, what is the contribution of your belief to your gender performance? |

| | |
|---|---|
| Female participant: | I think the first that comes to mind is I got my masters in nutrition education, and I worked for eight years with my degree. I had a good paying job, so it is very common in the US for men and woman to work, and to be successful regarding schools and jobs. Culturally speaking, there is a huge emphasis on the individual, and not on the community. Not even a family or a unit, but on individuals. So that is something I can see how influenced me, but I do not necessarily agree with it anymore. |
| Interviewer: | How does culturally defined gender performance affect your life in Turkey? |
| Male participant: | Think about, when we lived in İzmir, the perception of schools moms. |
| Female participant: | We both helped raise our kids. We know in Turkey that it is woman's job to raise the children, not the man's. The man would work or go to the tea house and come late hours, and the dinner would be ready, etc. For us, we share the roles of raising children; we share the roles of taking care of the house such as doing laundry and dishes. Especially, during the time I was ill, he stepped in and took care many things. Our Turkish friends that were moms, they did not understand. They were upset because they thought I was setting a bad example for their husbands. |
| Male participant: | That is what the men would say to me. They would say to my wife that she has her husband to help out, we don't have any help. |
| Interviewer: | Did you feel a sense of shame? |
| Male participant: | Not necessarily shame but discomfort. For me, it was unbalanced. Sometimes when we hosted our friends, when men see me cleaning or cooking, they would say that I was making them look bad. Almost every time the women would go up their husbands and tell 'Look, what he is doing!'. For the sake of not bringing shame on men but also I knew I needed to help my wife, that is the first thing that came to my mind about the level of my involvement in the house. This creates a fraction in the culture. |
| Interviewer: | Do you feel hindered in your code of dress such as wearing short for men or shorter clothes for women? |
| Female participant: | I dress differently here than in the US. It is to be more respectful. I do not want people to think I am a loose American woman. I am not kidding! There are some places where people might think I am a loose American woman. |
| Male participant: | It is not for her religion, it is the religion that's here. |

| | |
|---|---|
| Female participant: | I am not so modest that I am wearing clothes to my ankles and wrists. |
| Interviewer: | Would you have a different way of clothing in the US? |
| Female participant: | I would probably wear more shorts. |
| Interviewer: | What about you? (Referring to the male participant) |
| Male participant: | We live in the west part of the country where we have more freedom. The tension I am feeling with my dress code is that most men are working and in the places we tend to live there are professional men. So, I always look like I am on vacation and they always look like they are working. |
| Interviewer: | It has been said that suppression of men tend to create hidden lifestyles which in Islamic countries lead to unfaithful men cheating on their wives, illicit and incest relationship, and even same-sex interactions which all are dogmatically forbidden. There are even studies exploring the high levels of sexual abuse and illicit sex that is practiced in Islamic cultures. How do you protect yourself from situations that would cause you to have an interaction or conversation that would be considered unfaithfulness to you wife? How do you draw the boundaries of the public expression of sexuality as devoted Christian male in interaction with Muslim men and women? |
| Male participant: | In Christianity, I am also prescribed to avoid sexual immorality. We had young women living with us. She was our kid's teacher. We made a rule. If it is only her and me in the car, then she sits in the back seat. It is to avoid any appearance with her. She was even uncomfortable in the back seat, and I was uncomfortable riding her. For my American values, it is not a big deal, but we want to avoid the appearance of taking part in an adulterous sex, we asked her to ride in the back seat if we were alone in the car. |
| Interviewer: | So it is probably out of the fear of being subject to gossip. |
| Male participant: | It is biblical to avoid even the appearance of sin. Many times our children were asked 'who is this lady?' or 'Is that your mom?'. Just in general, coming from the US, it is a standard ministry practice not be alone with a woman. |
| Interviewer: | So is it more about your religion? |
| Male participant: | It is more about our religion than it is about culture. The culture here and there in the US share similarities. I inform my wife ahead of time in case I am with a woman so that it will not be any surprise to her when she hears from someone else. In America, when I was working outside the church, at a professional company, I could always avoid women during lunch but it is now different because the cultures are different. |

| | |
|---|---|
| Interviewer: | Have you ever come across an intercultural adaptation and integration issue stemming from your religious background? |
| Male participant: | During the sacrifice holiday when my neighbors bring me meat that has been sacrificed to Allah, even though the Bible gives me the freedom to eat it, I have been able to allow myself to cook and eat it. That is a cultural adaptation issue I have not been able to overcome because of my religion. There is many, I think. |
| Interviewer: | Can you come up with more examples of the situations where your dogmatic gender performance/perception of femininity and masculinity was challenged because of the predominant religious culture in your current country of residence? |
| Female participant: | Just as last week, there was a woman who lived in Turkey as a missionary. She was making a comment about that she was supposed to follow her husband, what she wanted did not matter, but she was submissively following her husband. So even among Christians in Turkey, there are different mindsets. We, as a family, live differently do not that. We see ourselves as a team, not just my husband making the decisions. We work and make decisions together. When it comes to ministry, we both have something to offer which equally as important. |
| Interviewer: | It is entirely the opposite here that men tend to make the decisions. |
| Male participant: | I remember once going to a bar with a Turkish friend, and we were meeting people he never met before. We were sitting and having a beer. They started to talk about making appointments with prostitutes. It is not because I was American I said no to this but it was because I was Christian I said no to this. |
| Interviewer: | So was your peer to peer interaction was challenged? |
| Male participant: | Yes, it was. It has been a couple of times with the same guy, and he was married at that time. We do not put our religion on people thinking that it is not a religion but a relationship. However, because of our religion, we may feel uncomfortable for what's been said or done. We used to live underneath a couple that fought all the time he would beat her, and that is more acceptable here. In America, it is more unacceptable first as a culture, secondly as Christians, we do not do it. |
| Female participant: | I have had quite a few moms who asked me if my husband beats me or yells at me, and they asked it very quietly. I know because we have seen it happen it even though many people do not accept it, it still happens. |

| | |
|---|---|
| Interviewer: | Do you both think these unfortunate situations where women are treated as inferior beings stem from the predominant religion? |
| Female participant: | Yes, I would agree with that. |
| Male participant: | Even a concept of paradise in the dominant religion here favors the men over women. I do not understand this. |

# Appendix B - Australian and American Missionary Couple

## Participants 2 (Male&Female Interviewees)

**Participant Background:** The participants are a married couple ministering as Christian missionaries in Turkey. The male participant is an Australian man born into a missionary family, and thus he spent many years abroad in an Asian country. He got his bachelors degree in multimedia studies at Central Queensland University and had many years of Christian ministry experience at various mission fields. The female participant is an American woman born into a Presbyterian community spending her childhood and youth in a highly religious and conservative environment away from all sorts of 'wordly' entertainments. She holds a bachelors degree in organizational communication from Northwest University.

## The Interview Transcription

| | |
|---|---|
| Interviewer: | Can you think of examples of religious deities and figures in your religious culture, which influenced your gender role and performance? (For instance, life of David or Jesus for men/ Mary and other biblical women figures) |
| Female participant: | Can I ask you a question. When you say our culture, does it have to be someone from our culture? Could we choose Jesus? |
| Interviewer: | I am interested in your culture which is American culture, and particularly your sub-culture where you grew up. It can be your religious community; you can give me a denomination name. |
| Female participant: | I grew up in a non-denominational church. After the age of eighteen probably someone who influenced my way of thinking is Mark Driscoll, he is from the Seattle area. |
| Interviewer: | What is his position? |
| Female participant: | The male is to be the protector of the female. He is to be the spiritual leader. A lot of responsibility relies on the male. |
| Interviewer: | Any biblical figure that influenced and shaped your gender role? |

| Female participant: | Probably a lot of writings of Paul. Specifically 1. Timothy 2:9, the verse about women being modest. That really shaped of my role as being a woman living and dressing in a modest way. |
| Interviewer: | Have you ever looked up to any of the Biblical woman figures? |
| Female participant: | Ruth. It was really bold of her to choose to leave her family to basically be a support to her mother in law and choose to follow her God, her religion, and give up her own. Mary who chose to sit at the feet of Jesus instead of Martha who was serving. |
| Interviewer: | Would you agree with the statement that the way you are right now, the way you perform your femininity, your gender identity which is also a female are all based on how you understand the Bible, all comes from the Biblical teachings? |
| Female participant: | Probably not entirely. I am sure there is some of it that were also influenced by my culture. For example, I can say that I grew up in a church where it was fine for women to teach and then later I learned other people interpret that verse differently. |
| Interviewer: | Which of the interpretations do you agree with at the moment? |
| Female participant: | I think it is fine for women to teach. I do not know if I personally would choose it, but it is not because I am female. I do not have anything against other females who could teach. |
| Interviewer: | What are some of the dogmatic areas that shaped your gender performance? In your own community back in Seattle, how was it like to be a woman there and to what extent was it influenced by church and the women in the church? Where does the woman that you are today come from? |
| Female participant: | Probably the huge majority of it comes from the examples I saw in my mother. |
| Interviewer: | Is she a believer? |
| Female participant: | Yes, she is. |
| Interviewer: | So a huge part of who she is comes from the Biblical teachings. Would you agree with that your gender is majorly and primarily influenced by Christianity and the Biblical texts? |
| Female participant: | Yes. |
| Interviewer: | Can you think of an existence of a woman outside the Biblical texts? |
| Female participant: | That I have been influenced by? Like someone who isn't a Christian? |
| Interviewer: | If there are areas where you do not really perform who you are based on the Bible, but on other things. |
| Female participant: | But gender specific? |

| | |
|---|---|
| Interviewer: | Yes, gender specific. The way you are sitting and talking is a woman thing. Your vocabulary and character, almost everything, are related to your gender. |
| Female participant: | (no answer) |
| Interviewer: | How about you (referring to the male participant)? What is the role of the Biblical teaching in your gender? |
| Male participant: | In Australian culture, there are some things that aren't Biblical. Men do not cry and do not show emotion; these are cultural. That is the weakness. In the religious culture, I think the religious culture is affected by that. Men do not feel like showing emotion even in religion. |
| Interviewer: | What about being superior to women? Outside the Christian culture, would you say you were meant to subdue women in Australian culture? Can we talk about gender equality? |
| Male participant: | People say there is equality, but there is this aspect of society that puts men higher. In terms of religious influence, some of John Piper's views on complementarianism like men and women compliment each other at different roles impact my perspective. |
| Interviewer: | Can you come up with some Biblical figures that influence the man you are today? |
| Male participant: | Abraham. The way how he was, in complete trust, he did not know where he was going, and how he was going to sacrifice his son in complete trust. |
| Interviewer: | Let's then think about Jesus's approach to both genders. I was discussing this very topic with an American guy, and he told me that the way Jesus behaved women really taught me how I should be behaving them. Would you say the man Jesus was influenced you? |
| Male participant: | Loving woman and showing them respect without making them a sexual taboo is important. The Bible also says treat younger women like your sister and older women as your mother. So it is very different from the world perspective. |
| Interviewer: | Let's think about the prophets and how they lived. When you read stories in which men were portrayed as responsible figures over women, did it teach you also to become responsible over women? |
| Male participant: | Yes, it did. |
| Female participant: | I thought of something. As a woman both in the US and Turkey, I feel very free to go up and ask people for help. Just saying in the US, if I had a problem with my car, I would go to a gas station, and I would ask the guy whatever he could find. Whereas most guys in my culture would not ask another person for help. |

| | |
|---|---|
| Interviewer: | From what I understand what you're saying for a woman to rely on men is okay whereas for a man to rely on a woman is not well appreciated. |
| Male participant: | To rely on someone in general. |
| Female participant: | I can ask a female or a male. Usually, I would ask guys because generally guys know more about cars than girls. If I was asking for directions, whether it is a girl who's closer or a guy who's closer, it would not matter. |
| Interviewer: | Is that challenged in here Turkey? |
| Female participant: | I think I am exactly the same here as far as that goes. |
| Interviewer: | In terms of cross-cultural communication at this point where you easily ask someone a question or ask for help is not very much challenged here? |
| Female participant: | No, it is not. |
| Interviewer: | Think about the way you perform your gender in your country of origin (how you lived as a woman or men) and compare it to other men or women here in your current country of residence. What are the differences and similarities? Above all, what is the contribution of your belief to your gender performance? |
| Female participant: | For me what's really important is loving others. In the US, it is probably the prime example of it, walking down the street any person that I pass, male or female, I would look at them in the eyes and smile and say hello. Here, if it is a woman, I would probably do the same, if it is a male I would not look at them. I would just walk past. |
| Interviewer: | Would you feel comfortable sitting or talking to a man in the US for which you do not feel as comfortable here in Turkey? |
| Female participant: | I do not think it makes a difference whether it is male or female, but I would feel uncomfortable because generally people in my area in the US might steal something from you or they are not hygienic. Here everybody uses transportation, so I feel much more comfortable sitting next to a woman than sitting next to a male depending on the age and his appearance. |
| Interviewer: | Can you compare how you lived as a man in Australia or where you grew up to the men here in Turkey? |
| Male participant: | What stands out the most is helping around the house. Even when I want to help clean the dishes away, the men would not do it here in Turkey. |
| Interviewer: | Have you ever been in a group of men where they talked about girls or visiting brothels? |

| | |
|---|---|
| Male participant: | Yes. They talked about girls in a degrading way. That is the sort of conversation that I do not like. It happens with young guys, and I try to change the conversation quickly. |
| Interviewer: | Think about the times when you went out to streets to meet guys and share your message with them. Did you find it difficult to initiate a conversation with them as your common interests differ from what's theirs? |
| Male participant: | I find it difficult approaching and engaging with an older man. There is an aspect of Turkish society where you have to respect the older men more than you would in Australia or the US. Here I need to let them have their say much more than I can speak. |
| Interviewer: | You cannot teach them. |
| Male participant: | Yes. They are trying to teach me all the time; I can only add here and there. |
| Female participant: | In relating male versus female, physical touch and eye contact are also very different here. I am much less likely to give any physical touch to a male here. Even a handshake. |
| Interviewer: | Would you say overall that your cross-cultural interactions with local here in Turkey are hinder and limited? |
| Female participant: | Not with women and probably so with men because I think in the US if I were to see a guy I did not know at all If I felt it I would just go and approach him. If I am here by myself and saw a guy, I would still approach, but it would be more difficult. There are so many cultural differences. The way they perceive me is different especially being here in Turkey as a foreigner. It also has changed the way I dress here. |
| Interviewer: | Have you ever come across an intercultural adaptation and integration issue stemming from your religious background? |
| Female participant: | I have changed overtime, but before I first came here when I did not know much about the culture, I ran into issues of being misunderstood or misperceived. I feel like the perception of male here when they see a foreigner female they would think I am easy to sleep with. |
| Interviewer: | But you are not because you are a Christian female. |
| Female participant: | Their perception of me because I am a Christian female is the same with the women they see in Hollywood because they are also Christian females. Since I chose the way I dress, It has not happened as much, but there are guys who want to touch me in an inappropriate way. Not knowing the local language much, it happened much frequently when I first came here. I did not know how to respond. For me, I highly value, because I am Christian, being modest both in the way I act and dress. I realize this culture is very different from |

American culture as far as what is perceived as modest. It has taken time for me to learn modestly in this culture, in a way that I feel comfortable and I can be perceived as someone who loves God.

Interviewer:          Have you ever been mocked on because of the way you dress up?

Female participant:   Yes, by other believers.

Interviewer:          So you were challenged in your own culture, which is the Christian church environment. Are you much appreciated here in the Muslim community because of your understanding of modesty including remaining chaste?

Female participant:   I think I was more appreciated and approved here than in the US.

Male participant:     When I talk to guys, if I lived in Istanbul for example where people sleep around, they expect me I would have also slept around. When I told them I never slept around, I stayed a virgin till I was married was a big shock. For a lot of young Turkish guys, they are supposed to experiment it.

Interviewer:          Do you think that affects your communication with other guys?

Male participant:     For some guys, I was the weird holy guy.

Interviewer:          What about your dress code?

Male participant:     I try to dress like other guys. It depends on the region; guys wear shorts in İzmir but in some parts they do not. I occasionally wear shorts.

Interviewer:          Compare to here, would you wear fewer shorts than in Australia?

Male participant:     It's less here. Because fewer people wear shorts here. For example, They cannot understand the reason why I did not have sex. Because I am a guy reaching out to Turks, they see me as a bigger threat than they see her a threat. In Turkey, they think men are a bigger threat.

Female participant:   I can give you an example. When I was walking in a neighborhood with a female friend of mine and people were friendly. However, as soon as they saw him walking by himself or with other men, they started to yell at him seeing him as a threat.

Male participant:     It was because I was an unknown guy. The girl removes the threat. They think guys are the threat; it is almost they consider guys as a second-class citizen.

# Appendix C - A German Protestant Pastor

## Participant 3

**Participant Background:** The participant is a German Christian pastor who has lived in Turkey for more than twenty years. He was born in Germany into a Reformed Christian community and got his degree in Theology. Among others, He planted the first international church in İzmir with his tremendous contribution to the local Christian community.

### The Interview Transcription

Interviewer: Can you think of examples of religious deities and figures in your religious culture which influenced your gender role and performance? (For instance, life of David or Jesus for men/Mary and other biblical women figures)

Participant: We have roles models like David. Of course, Jesus sets the best role model that I can have. I think He was the perfect role model.

Interviewer: How do you think these people influenced your gender representation? It could be in your relationship with your wife, as a father or a friend.

Participant: I think it influenced me in the way that Jesus treated women. Because this is different from what I was growing up. I thought of women as second-class people. When I became Christian, this view started to change, so I got a new perspective.

Interviewer: Think about the way you perform your gender in your country of origin (how you lived as a woman or men) and compare it to other men or women here in your current country of residence. What are the differences and similarities? Above all, what is the contribution of your belief to your gender performance?

Participant: Because I came here probably different from the general German would me. In general, still, the man was dominating. Even the emancipation was big. Still, the majority of men would be superior to women.

Interviewer: Is that how you lived in Germany?

Participant: Yes.

Interviewer: So you had the sense that you were superior to the opposite sex.

Participant: Yes.

Interviewer: How about here? How do you see men here?

Participant:     Here men are, even more, man's worth is double the woman. Outside the family, man is the king, but inside the family, it is a woman who rules the house. That is different what's in Germany.

Interviewer:     Would you say gender roles were pretty much equal in Germany whereas here there is a huge distinction between gender roles.

Participant:     Yes. At least in Germany it was equal. But here in society it is not even equal.

Interviewer:     Above all, what is the contribution of your belief to your gender performance? Would you separate your gender performance from your religious beliefs or would you say they are combined?

Participant:     I think they are combined. Looking at my role model who is Jesus, He was able to be a full man and take on the role of man in providing, caring, and loving that shows me how to be a real man, and how He treated other men is also important. Honoring men as much God gives every man his worth.

Interviewer:     Putting the religious doctrines of Jesus aside, I would like you to focus on how is your perception of an ideal man challenged here in Turkey?

Participant:     I think that the Turkish guys have quite a struggle with that. They are challenged with how they behave and talk. For example, a man helping his wife in the kitchen is challenging for him. I could easily accept the easier option.

Interviewer:     Do you feel like you become an outcast because of your gender performance, that you perform your gender role differently than local.

Participant:     Some people may just say he is a foreigner. They have distance anyway. They would not come closer. Maybe they are afraid they are being challenged.

Interviewer:     Do you think locals putting you in a box and defining you in limited definitions give you difficulty in living your daily life?

Participant:     It is easy to not accept that. People think we are foreigners and we do things differently.

Interviewer:     So it is an integration problem in a way.

Participant:     For them to accept, yes. It is always both sides. I have been affected by the culture as well. I have taken on from the culture some positive things that we do not have in our culture. The question is how much do I let myself be affected.

Interviewer:     Have you ever come across an intercultural adaptation and integration issue stemming from your religious background?

Participant:     It becomes a problem if people want me to do the things they are doing, that I do not agree. Like the traditions that have a background and that we do feel comfortable doing. For example, the henna night, we do not have it in Germany. However, if you look where it comes from and what's done with it, then it is a little bit problem to participate and do the same thing. When a baby is born, they sacrifice and animal and recite religious prayers. That is sometimes difficult.

Interviewer: Has anyone ever attempted to carry out a religious ceremony in your house? Did they give you demonic items that you refused?

Participant: Yes, they gave us an evil eye, and some guys did a religious prayer in our bathroom. Somebody even tried to do that in the church.

Interviewer: Is your code of dress same as it is in Germany?

Participant: When we first came here, no man was wearing shorts. It is a recent thing man is wearing shorts.

Interviewer: So it was a challenge for you because you wanted to wear shorts?

Participant: Yes, it was hot. I think the dress code is very important here. You have to clothe according to the professional role you have. It is a shame culture that this is so important to dress in a right mood. We have some Koreans at our church who told us that in their country if you are a teacher, you dress up like a teacher. Even when you take the garbage out, you still need to dress up like a teacher. I took this into consideration, especially while in the church to appropriately dress.

Interviewer: You said there is a shame culture here. What do you mean by that?

Participant: The greatest fear is that you do something other people would find unpleasant. The greatest fear is losing faith, and this is very important to keep the faith. People think what their neighbors think is good emphasizing someone else's opinion.

Interviewer: Would you say that you come from a culture of honor.

Participant: Not really. It was not a strong thing in my life. However, it is a culture where people are valued. If you go to a doctor in Germany, they give you value. Because it is a Christian culture, therefore the culture is affected by it.

Interviewer: So you background culture is being challenged here in Turkey.

Participant: Yes.

Interviewer: I have a question for you as to gender binary. Would you explain share your ideas on it?

Participant: I believe is that God made man and woman as each one special. God gave each one different task in life. They are different beings at the end, so we need both sides. If we blur this, then we do not have either man or woman.

Interviewer: So there is no way if one wants to change her gender?

Participant: Yes.

Interviewer: In this sense, there is no challenge for you because that is exactly what is believed in Islam.

Participant: They believe it but still there are lots of homosexual and transsexual activities under cover.

Interviewer: What about seeing transvestites freely walking and working in the streets? Does it challenge you to see them?

Participant: I am challenged to pray for them. Because each one has a history and each one has lived and experienced things that have helped them to be where they are.

# Appendix D - An American Methodist Missionary

## Participant 4

**Participant Background:** The participant is an American Christian missionary residing in Turkey. She has a Bachelor of Science in Elementary Education from Bob Jones University. She comes from a conservative Methodist church background. She seeks to continually develop strong relationships with local Muslims.

### The Interview Transcription

Interviewer: Can you think of examples of religious deities and figures in your religious culture which influenced your gender role and performance? (For instance, life of David or Jesus for men/Mary and other biblical women figures)

Participant: I think a character that has helped affect my perception of gender roles is Mary Magdalena. She gave up everything to follow Jesus. She is the woman who inspired me to be who I am. Also Deborah. She was married and was an active figure in Biblical history. They were brave and strong. They were not held back because they were girls.

Interviewer: Think about the way you perform your gender in your country of origin (how you lived as a woman or men) and compare it to other men or women here in your current country of residence. What are the differences and similarities? Above all, what is the contribution of your belief to your gender performance?

Participant: I think I grew up with the idea like I could do whatever I want. There are two different things about the way I group up. One is the side which is the American way of life saying it does not matter if you are a girl or boy. You want to be whom you want to be, you could be the president of the United States. However, at home, my brothers could go to boy scout camps and play with fire. Girls were taught to be at home so we learned how to make a cake.

Interviewer: You had certain roles in the household you grew up in such as girls were meant to deal with chores whereas men would go out for hunting and do the man thing. Would you say there was a huge distinction between gender roles?

| | |
|---|---|
| Participant: | I never wanted to go down the road and wanted to be like other girls. My favorite toy growing up was a gun. |
| Interviewer: | Were you allowed to play with a guy? |
| Participant: | Yes, I was. I was also wearing skirts because I liked them. |
| Interviewer: | Did you have the feeling that you should not be playing with a gun? |
| Participant: | I felt quite free to do it, but a part of it was because I was a little girl. In my house, it would not last forever. My dad was the great winner, and my mom depended on him. Even when she wanted to write e-mails, she would ask my dad. I recently noticed that she hides behind my dad in many ways. If someone invites her out for lunch, she could ask my dad. In Turkey, there are many similarities. |
| Interviewer: | So you grew up in a family where your dead was superior to your mom. |
| Participant: | Yes. |
| Interviewer: | Did it come from their understanding of the Biblical teachings? |
| Participant: | I do not know. It could be a personal thing. |
| Interviewer: | Are they pious people? |
| Participant: | Yes. It is because of my dad's understanding of the Bible for sure. He believed that man is the head of the house. Sometimes my dad, just to show that he is superior, would make a decision all by himself. Looking at married Turkish couples, I see many similarities. My married female friends cannot really do anything without asking their husbands. |
| Interviewer: | Does it have to do with Islam? |
| Participant: | I could come from Islam. I assume that Turkish people claim to be Muslims so where else could it be coming from? |
| Interviewer: | Let's talk about your dress code. Were you challenged back in the US? Were you wearing jeans in the US? |
| Participant: | I was wearing jeans in highschool. I had to wear skirts at my university. After I graduated, I did not want to wear skirts anymore. When I moved to Turkey in 2010, I came here like how a typical American girl would look like. |
| Interviewer: | Why did you change your dress code then? Do you feel more integrated dressing up like this? |
| Participant: | I was told by my friends that I would have to change my dress code. I feel more comfortable in skirts now. |
| Interviewer: | Are there areas in your life that cause you difficulty because you perform your gender differently than the locals? For example, approaching or making an eye contact with men. |
| Participant: | Eye contact and even touching, I would avoid all of these here, not necessarily in the US. |
| Interviewer: | Do you face problems because you are a white American girl living in Turkey? |
| Participant: | Maybe not. Because I am tall. |

| | |
|---|---|
| Interviewer: | So is your height an advantage for you? |
| Participant: | It is an advantage if I want people to stare at me which I am okay with. In fact, I do not talk to men. |
| Interviewer: | One reason why I dress like this is to avoid affairs with men. |
| Participant: | This justifies your dress code. |
| Interviewer: | How about in the church you are attending? Would you feel more comfortable with men in the church? |
| Participant: | I think I talk to them a little bit more but I do not look at them in the eyes. I also dress the same in the church. |
| Interviewer: | Just because you have your faith in common with the men in the church, this makes you feel more comfortable. |
| Participant: | Slightly. Not much comfortable. They start getting too friendly, and I do not like this. That is why I keep distance. |
| Interviewer: | Have you ever come across an intercultural adaptation and integration issue stemming from your religious background? |
| Participant: | My religious background actually helps me adapt because I was very religious. It is very normal for me here. |
| Interviewer: | In which sense does your religious background in the US make you feel more comfortable here? |
| Participant: | I went to a very religious university with a very strict dress code. We had to go to the chapel and the prayer room every day. I went to Bob Jones University. He was a very religious Methodist preacher. If your skirt were an inch short, I would go into the merits and people would just look at you and the judgmental spirit was all over the place. I came to Turkey, and I felt normal. |
| Interviewer: | Do you feel more comfortable talking to veiled women in Turkey? |
| Participant: | Not really. I try to talk to everybody. I wear skirts because this is who I am. |
| Interviewer: | I know you come from a background where chastity for women was highly appreciated and encouraged. Moving here, how do you see yourself fitting in the community in this context? |
| Participant: | I fit quite nicely. I get the feeling that it is very important for women in Turkey too. |
| Interviewer: | Above all, what would be the contribution your religion to your gender performance if you had to rate it? |
| Participant: | It is probably one hundred percent. |
| Interviewer: | Have you ever thought about other gender identities? |
| Participant: | No, I did not. |

# Appendix E - A Feminist Theologian and Biblical Scholar

## Participant 6

**Participant Background:** The participant is a former dean at an Australian university and an associate professor of Biblical Studies, specializing in hermeneutics and Old Testament studies. Her publications include *Them, Us and Me: How the Old Testament Speaks to People Today*, *Raising Women Leaders*, and *Three's A Crowd: Pentecostalism, Hermeneutics, and the Old Testament*. She regularly speaks at international events and has appeared on multiple national TV and radio programs in Australia, including the ABC TV's Q&A program. She is currently the President of the Society for Pentecostal Studies and is part of the steering committee for Biblical Ethics in the Society of Biblical Literature. Her research interests include Pentecostal hermeneutics, prophetic literature and feminist readings of Scripture.

### The Interview Transcription

| | |
|---|---|
| Interviewer: | Can you think of examples of religious deities and figures in your religious culture which influenced your gender role and performance? (For instance, life of David or Jesus for men/Mary and other biblical women figures) |
| Participant: | One of the big things that took me a long time to work through within Christianity is the understanding God as the father. God is presented as a father, so it is kind of like God is male. It is only many years of studying that I began to see that God is not male, that is just one of many terms we use for God. However, that almost has become the only way to refer to God. In one sense, for me, it was very liberating to discover in the Bible that there are also feminine ways to refer to God and the idea that God is a mother is very much in the Old Testament prophets and their poetry. There are quite positive mother images in the Bible, but we do not discuss at the church level, it is only through the academic study that I began to discover and explore the different understandings of who God is. The idea of who God is in my home culture is very much a masculine idea. For |

a woman to look up to as role models within the Biblical texts are particularly the ones in the Old Testament such as Deborah in the Book of Judges. She was a judge, prophet, and leader to Israel. Even Esther capitulated the culture in her time. She was courageous, and her decisions were brave which is very inspirational. There are also women in the New Testament particularly in the Book of Acts like Priscilla. Also, Lydia who was a leader in the early church. These women were teachers and were very instrumental in the establishment of the early church. These are the Biblical figures I look up to as role models. There is also Mary whom I look up to even though I did not look up to her when I was younger probably because of the fear factor or just a misunderstanding of the role of Mary in Catholicism that we avoided Mary as a role model. However, it is only later in life I have come to see Her as a role model.

Interviewer:    Think about the way you perform your gender in your country of origin (how you lived as a woman) and compare it to other men or women here in your current country of residence. What are the differences and similarities? Above all, what is the contribution of your belief to your gender performance?

Participant:    Some differences that are quite obvious are in the communication style. Even the interactions among the genders in Australia were much more demonstrative, and it is a lot more equal. So it is nothing to give a hug to a man who is a friend. Sometimes in church culture, they can be funny about it but in the church culture I grew up in we gave everyone a kiss and hug. In Turkey, it is a lot more conservative. You kiss women, but with men, you shake hands. It is quite visible even when my niece was visiting; it is quite obvious to us this element of interaction. Not just in greetings however, in general communication, I do not know if that's because I am trying to be too culturally sensitive, but I am very careful about talking to men that I do not tend to men that much over here because I have the idea that it is not normal or it could be taken the wrong way. It could be seen as loose and free. I am very reserved, and I do not talk to men that often that I encounter.

Interviewer:    As one of my research questions suggest, in the context of intercultural communication, would you say this particular issue of having less interaction with men has become a hindering point in your communication?

Participant:    Yes. Because I am not quite sure what to do. I tend to hesitate, and I wait to respond. I have taken a very passive role whereas in Australia I would be much more active in being an initiator in conversations or interactions. I am not an initiator here. Even I observe other women; I do not see many women initiating many conversations. It seems like in public settings or general interactions, women are a lot more passive and deferring to men. If men say something, women would stop speaking and defer to men. Even with educated people, I see that women defer to men in conversations. It has some implications for my role, how I see myself. I do not want to offend people and be culturally insensitive which leads to hesitancy, and that is also a hinderance.

Interviewer: So your religious culture in general interactions is being challenged here in a negative way.

Participant: Yes.

Interviewer: You are a scholar and a professor. So you have been in academia for long years. You have been exposed to the concepts discussed in my research. How would you position yourself as being a Christian woman yet being an academic scholar? Would you say gender performance, despite all the academic researches you have made, was still shaped by your religious background?

Participant: I think that within the broader secular world, I do not find any limitations for being a woman and my religious background. My religious background is that men and women are created equal and that men and women are equally gifted in whatever the role is. Other groups in Christianity do not believe that. For me, there is no issue to have a leadership role within academic setting and teaching or administrative role.

Interviewer: Your perception of men and women is equal just as the seculars would suggest.

Participant: However, working with other Christian colleagues that are conservative, that does become an issue. Not a limitation but it has been awkward working with them. I know that they are not comfortable with me as a woman. Particularly because I was acting as the dean of the college. In the position of authority, it would be uncomfortable seeing me as equal.

Interviewer: I hypothesize that no matter how educated you are, we are still subconsciously led and directed by our perception of the supreme. Do you support this idea?

Participant: Yes, I would. Because I am an academic person, I interacted with the secular. I do not know what their religious backgrounds are. They would say they are spiritual but not religious. That is very much reflected in the interaction. Whereas I had some interactions with an imam so he would say that I was a woman with lower status. I was told that my interactions should be with women so very much division of genders.

Interviewer: You do not compromise your belief to reach certain academic level, do you?

Participant: I try not to. I do not think so. I do not try to downplay my gender within the academic world.

Interviewer: Do you find it oppressive to be always led by a set of religious belief that are rather under the surface while being in the academic world interacting with others?

Participant: I do not. I see it as a worldview and ethical way of thinking. So for me, like the religion is not just a weight around my neck but glasses through I view the world.

Interviewer: Have you ever come across an intercultural adaptation and integration issue stemming from your religious background?

Participant: I am very aware of being more conservative in dress. I would say in İzmir it is pretty similar, but in other parts of Turkey, it is much more different.

Interviewer: Do you find it a negative thing when you had to adapt to the regional dress code?

Participant: Yes. I do not know if I would call it a negative thing, but I am much more aware of being conservative in clothing trying not to be obviously western. Because that draws negative attention.

Interviewer: So your position as a western Christian woman is negatively challenged here regarding dress code or your relationships with others.

Participant: Definitely challenged with interactions and communication.

# Appendix F - A Haitian Pentecostal Christian

## Participant 7

**Participant Background:** The participant is a Haitian woman living in Turkey. She worked at her local church in Haiti. She learned Turkish and studied chemistry at a Turkish university. She was born into a conservative black Christian community being raised according to the local Christian traditions that differ from the western practice of Christianity.

## The Interview Transcription

**Interviewer:** Can you think of examples of religious deities and figures in your religious culture which influenced your gender role and performance? (For instance, life of David or Jesus for men/Mary and other biblical women figures)

**Participant:** They used to tell me examples of Mary or Esther. Since my name is Esther, my mom used to say that 'your name is Esther. Why don't you live like the real queen you are?' and you know Esther is a queen. When I was nine years old, even my pastor told the same. I was acting in a play, and I was the Mary figure in the play. Since then, everybody used to call me Mary. So, I have to be very careful with what I am doing. I was like a model in the church. I did not have the chance to make mistakes. I had to be a model.

**Interviewer:** How are these religious figures influenced your gender performance? For instance, Esther of the Bible stands out to be a brave woman and faithful. Which kind of attributes of these women influenced your gender expression?

**Participant:** I was fighting with myself. I knew I had to be the certain way, not because I wanted it but because of people who had expectations on me. Everybody believed in me. I was fighting with myself. Because I did not want to disappoint them.

**Interviewer:** Would you say, in the context of chastity, according to the Catholic texts, seeing Mary in her full virginity also affected the way you preserved yourself?

**Participant:** Of course. In Haiti, some girls got pregnant at early ages. In my family, going out with boys and engaging with them were forbidden.

**Interviewer:** So for girls to go out at night was forbidden?

| | |
|---|---|
| Participant: | Yes, it was forbidden. I had a boyfriend, but I could not talk about it to my family and pastor. It took the world war to confess them I love someone. We used to have prayer times in the church. Whenever I was attending the meeting, I was going with my family. But when I was friendly simply chilling and having fun, everybody was staring at us and thinking nastily. |
| Interviewer: | You and I agree on the fact that your gender identity was immensely influenced by your religious upbringing. |
| Participant: | Of course. |
| Interviewer: | Think about the way you perform your gender in your country of origin (how you lived as a woman or men) and compare it to other women here in your current country of residence. What are the differences and similarities? Above all, what is the contribution of your belief to your gender performance? |
| Participant: | Since I have been here eight years, I cannot really see the difference. Because of the dogmas, I think it is not the same everywhere. The church was like a village for us in a sense that everybody knew each other. Everybody had a say on me. I was like in prison. |
| Interviewer: | Coming here has been liberating for you. |
| Participant: | Yes. I was looking for my freedom. That's why I came here. I resigned from all my duties at the church where I was taking after children. I was also working with a missionary group. |
| Interviewer: | There was so much pressure on you that you were held back in your gender expression. You decided to move abroad to liberate yourself. |
| Participant: | Yes, to some extent. |
| Interviewer: | Would you say women are much freer here? |
| Participant: | No. First I came to Ankara, I was almost dying. When I was wearing a skirt, everybody was looking at me as though I was naked. I had to be careful in what I was doing. |
| Interviewer: | Do you think this is an Islamic influence? |
| Participant: | Yes. |
| Interviewer: | So, your dress code was restricted here? |
| Participant: | Yes. Because in our culture, if you were a believer, you could not wear jeans. |
| Interviewer: | What about wearing jewelry in your own culture? Did you grow up in a Pentecostal church? |
| Participant: | Yes, unfortunately. Jewellery was not much appreciated. |
| Interviewer: | Coming to Turkey, what is the contribution of your faith to your gender performance here? As a woman, do you act on your belief or you separate your gender representation from your beliefs? |
| Participant: | Coming here really helped me to fix my relationship with God. Because I am here alone which means I can do whatever I want. There is no pressure on me including family. Sometimes, I make mistakes, |

but nobody judges me here for things I do wrong. I know what to do and what not do. I can choose what is better for me.

Interviewer: So, you do not really include your beliefs in your gender performance and live your woman side separately than your faith.

Participant: Yes, exactly.

Interviewer: Have you ever come across an intercultural adaptation and integration issue stemming from your religious background?

Participant: I used to live with Muslim girls. I will give you an example which really hurt me. When we cooked home, we cooked together. But every time I cooked, they would say things like they were not hungry. One time, one veiled girl was speaking ill of me, and I overheard the whole conversation. They did not eat on purpose thinking that the food I give them would be as if they were getting food from a pig. They did not get my food because I am Christian. After all, I heard, I asked them to repeat what they said behind me and they told me that they do not eat with Christians. They told me that I was not clean enough to eat with.

Interviewer: Do you think they thought you were not clean because you are a black person?

Participant: I do not think they were talking about my blackness because they were referring to my religion. Sitting with me was insulting for them.

Interviewer: What about the fact that you are a Christian woman? Do you think men stare at you in sexual ways?

Participant: Of course. They stare at me all the time. Because I am a Christian woman, they think I am easy to be with. They even offered me money to have sex with them.

Interviewer: Do you think in Islamic countries black Christian women are seen as sexual objects?

Participant: Yes. I am not a slut.

Interviewer: Can you mention the distinctive masculine and feminine roles in the black Christian culture you come from? Is the expression of both genders fluid or quite divided?

Participant: We expect men to behave like a man and women be like how a woman would be like. The men had the final say, but the women workers at my church actively participated in church governance.

www.ingramcontent.com/pod-product-compliance
Lightning Source LLC
Chambersburg PA
CBHW050656270326
41927CB00012B/3048